MW00423994

SISTERS AND BROTHERS
All These Years

SISTERS AND BROTHERS
All These Years

*Taking Another Look at the
Longest Relationship in Your Life*

Lillian S. Hawthorne

VanderWyk & Burnham

Copyright © 2003 by Lillian S. Hawthorne

Published by VanderWyk & Burnham
A Division of Publicom, Inc.
P.O. Box 2789, Acton, Massachusetts 01720

All rights reserved. No part of this book may be reproduced or transmitted in any form or by any means without permission in writing from the publisher, except in the case of brief quotations embodied in critical articles or reviews with appropriate citation. Address correspondence to Permissions, VanderWyk & Burnham, P.O. Box 2789, Acton, MA 01720-6789.

This publication is sold with the understanding that the publisher is not engaged in rendering legal, medical, psychiatric, or other professional services. If expert assistance is required, the services of a competent professional person should be sought.

This book is available for quantity purchases. For information on bulk discounts, call (800) 789-7916 or write to Special Sales at the above address.

Library of Congress Cataloging-in-Publication Data
Hawthorne, Lillian S., 1924–
    Sisters and brothers all these years : taking another look at the longest relationship in your life / Lillian S. Hawthorne.
        p. cm.
    Includes index.
    ISBN 1-889242-19-5 (soft cover)
    1. Aged—Family relationships. 2. Brothers and sisters. I. Title.

HQ1061 .H3765 2003
306.875—dc21

                                2002034920

Cover and interior book design by Publicom, Inc.
Cover photograph courtesy of David Jacobs and Bena Rogoff

FIRST PRINTING
Manufactured in the United States of America
10 9 8 7 6 5 4 3 2 1

To Bea

Always my big sister,
as long as love and
memory will last

contents

Preface   ix
Introduction   1

part one

SIBLINGS: THE SPECIAL RELATIONSHIP

chapter 1
Who Are Siblings? What Are Siblings?   9
chapter 2
Childhood Siblings: In the Beginning   17
chapter 3
Adult Siblings: The Great Divide   31

part two

SIBLINGS: THE LASTING RELATIONSHIP

chapter 4
Aging Siblings: The Last Chance   47
chapter 5
The Siblings' Stories   55
chapter 6
The Sisters   63
chapter 7
The Brothers   83
chapter 8
The Sisters and Brothers   101
chapter 9
Finding Our Siblings, Losing Our Siblings   119

Appendix
Building Bridges with Your Siblings   133
Index   135

$\mathcal{I}$ grew up as one of two siblings. As children, my sister and I were neither especially alike or close nor were we especially dissimilar or distant. We simply knew we were sisters, and we took our relationship for granted, scarcely giving any thought to what that relationship meant.

As married adults, we lived far apart from each other. We kept in touch during those years through letters, phone calls, and most recently, e-mails. We remembered each other's birthdays, anniversaries, the births of our children, their accomplishments, and the births of our grandchildren.

We also visited each other periodically. During the earlier years, these were family visits with our parents and all of our children present, so there was little opportunity for private time together. During the later years, when our parents were gone and our children had moved away, we did have time for personal visits and talks together, just the two of us. Over that time, I noticed that the conversations seemed to shift from wondering about our families' futures to sharing memories of our own past. Even if we disagreed about things, the more we spoke with each other, the closer we felt.

Then a few years ago, we each began to have health problems, although mine were far milder than my sister's. She experienced two minor heart attacks, and when I visited her afterwards, she seemed increasingly frail, quiet, and preoccupied—almost as if she were slowly beginning to slip away.

Two years ago, my sister suffered a major heart attack, and for the first time, the prognosis was guarded. I made arrangements to fly out to see her, but on the evening before I was scheduled to depart, the hospital called to inform me that my sister had lapsed into a coma and was not expected to last the night. I was told that, if I wished, the telephone could be placed next to her ear so I could speak to her. The caller assured me that hearing was the last sense to go, and that words spoken could be heard almost until the last few moments before death.

So I spoke to my sister that evening. I told her that I would be with her the very next day. I hoped she could wait for me, but if not, I wanted her to know that I loved her and I was glad we were sisters. It turned out that she did not, could not, wait for me; but I believe, or I want to believe, that she did hear those last words I spoke to her.

At her funeral, I looked around and saw her

husband, her children, her grandchildren, and her friends there. But I realized that I was the one who had known her the longest. I was the only one who had shared and experienced the moments that made up her earliest memories.

Afterward, as so often happens following a funeral, I began to reflect a great deal, not only about my sister and myself but also about other siblings our age and their experiences with each other during their lifetimes. I observed and spoke to many older siblings; I asked questions and encouraged them to tell their stories, to share their remembrances of their sisters and brothers. I was struck by how willingly and unguardedly they spoke, as if these were experiences and feelings they had long wanted to discuss but somehow, until now, hadn't had the opportunity or permission to do so.

The seed for this book was planted by those many different stories, and, from them, grew to have shape, purpose, and meaning. It is my hope that this book may be not only for siblings in my own generation but also for siblings in the younger adult generations, so that they can come to understand what it means to be "sisters and brothers all these years."

SISTERS AND BROTHERS
All These Years

This book is about sibling relationships in our older years. Sibling relationships in general are among the earliest and the most lasting relationships in our lives, but they are also among the least understood and the most underestimated.

For the better part of the twentieth century, most of the attention and literature on siblings focused on childhood, and this was usually within the context of Freudian theories of sibling rivalry. As a result, the most common vision of siblings was one of children competing with each other, literally or symbolically, for some parental prize or praise. Concern or consideration about one's siblings seemed to stop after childhood, as if the relationship had ended.

Perhaps we assumed that whatever relationship was formed in childhood simply persisted throughout life. Certainly, this assumption would be partly true because many of the primary patterns formed in those early years do last in some way over time. However, part of it would be untrue because we know that people can and do—in fact, sometimes must—change with changed circumstances. Perhaps we assumed that once past childhood, siblings were not central to or even relevant in each other's lives. Again, this would be partly true because in their adult years, siblings generally lead separate and different lives. But, again, part of this assumption would be untrue because siblings are still siblings when they grow up, when they grow older, even when they grow apart. The connection among them continues whether sisters and brothers are physically present or not.

Recently, more studies have been conducted about adult sibling relationships. This may well be due to the looming presence of baby boomers. Members of this generation have now entered their own middle age, which means that they are beginning to experience the failings and deaths of their parents. This has made them more concerned about, and more in need of, their peers as survivors and supports—after all, siblings were their first, if not necessarily their closest, peers.

Still, there has been little serious attention paid to the relationships of aging siblings in their fifties, sixties, seventies, eighties, or even older. With people's longevity increasing so markedly, sibling relationships are lasting longer. As a result, aging siblings have become more noticeable, and their greater visibility is commanding greater attention. You may have read and enjoyed the autobiographical stories of the remarkable Delaney sisters, who experienced life together side by side for more than one hundred years, but this was more an interesting phenomenon than a representative portrait. What is it that really happens to the relationships among aging brothers and sisters? How does the aging process and the ever-present shadow of mortality affect these relationships?

It is the message of this book that siblings play a unique and continuing, although changing, role in our lives. This role is no less important in our later years than it was in our earlier years. In fact, the aging process may actually make our sibling relationships more special than ever because it brings the final opportunity to heal any hurts of the past and to recognize the reality that remains. The importance of this life process, of review and reconciliation, is recorded in professional literature on aging and is reflected in the personal stories of aging siblings themselves.

Sisters and Brothers All These Years presents in two parts the unique, continuing role of siblings. In part 1, "Siblings: The Special Relationship," the focus is on the general knowledge available on siblings, and this general knowledge is provided as foundation. In part 2, "Siblings: The Lasting

Relationship," the focus is specifically on siblings in their later years.

Part 1, chapter 1 presents an overview of some of the common perceptions, stereotypes, contradictions, and ambiguities about siblings. Chapter 2 describes childhood sibling relationships—where it all begins, when it all begins, how it all begins. Chapter 3 discusses the relationships in adulthood, when siblings can be furthest apart from each other geographically, personally, socially, and emotionally.

The second part begins with chapter 4, which describes some of the major changes that the aging process can bring and how these changes can affect sibling relationships. Chapters 5, 6, 7, and 8 relate the personal stories and experiences of different groups of aging siblings, including "The Sisters," "The Brothers," and "The Sisters and Brothers." These people are real, and their stories are true, though names and minor details have been altered to protect confidentiality. The particular groupings in the chapters are not intended to imply any particular significance or priority but to provide some structure to the stories.

The siblings in these interviews ranged in age from late sixties (the youngest was 68) to early nineties (the oldest was 93); most were clustered in the seventies. There were more women than men, probably reflecting the preponderance of older women in the larger society. All of the brothers and sisters interviewed were biological siblings (none came from divorced or remarried parents, and none had half siblings or stepsiblings). Most of those who were in their eighties had already experienced the death of at least one sibling.

The women tended to speak more readily and fully about their feelings toward their siblings than did the men. The men preferred to talk more about activities or behaviors. Both the women and the men were quite comfortable talking about their past relationships with their siblings. In fact, they tended to interweave their memories of the past with their accounts of the present.

Chapter 9, the final chapter, is titled "Finding Our Siblings, Losing Our Siblings." The focus here is on the dual task in our later years of trying to reconnect with our siblings while trying to cope with our own mortality and theirs.

The sources for the material in this book are many and varied, direct and indirect, professional and personal. These include research and readings on the aging process in general and on sibling relationships in general; my own professional training and experience in counseling older people; observations of and personal acquaintances with aging siblings; and interviews with various older brothers and sisters.

The final source is my own life experience as an older person and as an aging sibling. Over the years I have come to learn that, as siblings, we are important but imperfect people in each other's lives. Yet, whether we want it or not, there is more that binds us together than breaks us apart.

part one

Siblings:

the

Special

Relationship

chapter one

WHO ARE SIBLINGS? WHAT ARE SIBLINGS?

*I*t is estimated that approximately 80 percent of all people in the United States today have siblings. Given so many brothers and sisters, it makes sense that we should try to understand who and what siblings are.

We know that our siblings are our parents' other children, who once shared our home and who still share our heredity. But this definition is no longer sufficient, considering today's variations of parental arrangements through divorce, remarriage, blended families, and so on. As a result, there may be stepsiblings, half siblings, or adopted siblings, people who share only some, or sometimes even none, of the same heritage.

As adults, we most likely have in-law siblings— the siblings of our spouses and the spouses of our siblings—who share neither our homes nor our histories and are only connected to us through the other people in our lives. If trying to define *who* siblings are has become so complicated, trying to understand *what* siblings are has become almost elusive.

MYTHS AND MESSAGES

Are siblings supposed to be virtually our clones, to have similar qualities, lifestyles, and personalities to ours because of similar heredity and upbringing? After all, they are the only other people in the world who shared the same place and parents, heard the same stories, ate the same foods, learned the same lessons. Certainly we can recognize parts of ourselves in our siblings, but we also know from observation or perhaps personal experience the many ways in which we are not alike or are even opposite. Indeed, we are constantly surprised by how different from us our siblings can be.

Are siblings supposed to be good friends who share activities and interests and enjoy each other's company? We know that may not be so either. Certainly siblings can be friendly, yet not be our friends in the way that others are. Sibling closeness is not the same as "best friendship." Even when siblings act less than friendly, the relationship is still more than a friendship. We voluntarily select or reject our friends for various reasons or needs at certain times in our lives. But we do not get to choose our siblings or even to choose whether to have siblings at all. Nor can we ever really lose the relationship, even though we may want to, try to, or think that we have.

Are siblings supposed to be merely relatives, to be just like other members of the family? If so, why is it that the relationship can become so emotionally charged, positively or negatively? Why is it that so often the attachments, the joys, the hurts, and the losses that siblings cause us to feel reach so much deeper, and our reactions toward them are so much stronger than with other relatives, even in similar situations? Why is it that siblings can please us more and hurt us more than others can, and that the absence of a relationship with them can be just as powerful as its presence?

Even if we really don't know *what* siblings are, we do have a vague but deeply felt sense of what we want our relationship with them to be. We use expressions such as "She was like a sister to me" and "We could have been brothers." These words seem to hold a kind of wistful longing for perfect closeness—and even though we seem unable to define specifically what we mean, we keep looking for and hoping to find that closeness in our siblings.

This idealized vision of the sibling relationship is in contrast or perhaps in reaction to the kinds of images and messages we receive from popular writings about siblings. As children, we meet the prototype sibling figures of the wicked stepsisters in the Cinderella story. As young-adult readers, we encounter stories about brothers and sisters who are difficult, who disagree or are disappointed with each other. In adult novels, we read about romantic triangles or career contests involving siblings. In history books, from ancient empires to modern times, we read about siblings who plot against each other, wage war against each other, and even destroy each other for power or control.

In the Bible, the book of Genesis is filled with stories of dysfunctional sibling relationships. It includes the account of the first human murder—Cain's murder of his brother Abel because of jealousy over God's acceptance of Abel's sacrifice. There is the story about treachery and deception between the twins Jacob and Esau over inheriting the paternal blessing and family leadership. And there is the account of violence and revenge taken by Joseph's brothers because of their father's favoritism toward Joseph.

Rarely do novelists, storytellers, biographers, or historians present strong, positive pictures of siblings as role models, allies, protectors, or simply as sources of a different kind of family attachment.

Until recently, psychiatrists viewed sibling relationships almost entirely through the prism of the Freudian concept of sibling rivalry. This concept was presumed to be universal and inevitable in child-

hood and perhaps, though not necessarily, sublimat-
ed in adulthood. Thanks to Freud, the terms *sibling*
and *rivalry* became virtually attached to each other.

In spite of all this, or perhaps because of it, we
continue to seek in our siblings some kind of fantasized, perfect attachment—and we do so in vain. The
irony, of course, is that both the negative images we
read about and the idealized notions we dream about
obscure the realities of what siblings actually are or
can be.

COMPLICATIONS
AND CONNECTIONS

Sibling relationships are complicated, ambivalent,
powerful, and lasting. They are all of these characteristics at the same time, and each characteristic
interrelates with and reinforces the others.

• • •

COMPLICATED The sibling relationship in general is quite complicated and sometimes even contradictory. For example, it is *involuntary* (because we
do not choose to be a sibling nor do we choose our
particular siblings) at the same time as it is *voluntary*
(because we can choose the contacts we make and the
connections we have with each other).

Because so many people have siblings, the relationship is *common,* yet because each relationship has its own inimitable story, it is *unique.* We may have more than one sibling or more than one kind of sibling, but none of these relationships can be interchanged or replicated.

It is *persistent* because it lasts all of our lives, yet it is *not* (necessarily) *consistent* because it changes at different times in our lives.

Because our siblings are on the same peer level as we are, they do not really have authority or power over us, but the relationship itself is powerful. There may be people in our lives whom we know better or like better, yet there are certain ties that exist only with our siblings and not with anyone else in the world.

• • •

AMBIVALENT The sibling relationship is a deeply ambivalent relationship—we want different, sometimes opposing, things from our siblings, and these needs and desires are as real as they are conflicting.

We want togetherness and connection with each other, but we also want separateness and independence.

We want to have things in common, but we also want to have things that are uniquely our own.

We want our siblings to like us and perhaps be like us, but we also want to be different from them or better than them (smarter, prettier, thinner, more successful, and so on).

We want to know that we could help each other in times of need, but we don't want to have to need them.

We also feel different, sometimes opposing, emotions about our siblings. Again, these exist at the same time, and all are genuine. We feel friendship and frustration, love and pain, pride and disappointment; we feel close yet also distant. It is an intimate and personal relationship filled with unquestionable and probably unavoidable ambivalences.

• • •

POWERFUL The sibling relationship is one of potentially three immediate blood relationships in our lives. It has great power because we and our siblings are connected to each other with what has been called genetic glue. The three familial relationships—with our siblings, our parents, and our children—are irrevocable and irreplaceable. A person can be an ex-spouse, ex-friend, or ex-lover, but not an ex-sibling, ex-child, or ex-parent.

Our feelings toward and about our siblings, whether positive or negative, are stronger and more enduring than they are toward others not connected by this invisible but unbreakable bond. It is difficult to say whether the sibling relationship is emotionally charged because it is so powerful, or whether the emotional intensity is what makes the relationship so powerful—

it's probably both. Indeed, we are often surprised by the unexpected power of the relationship and sometimes realize this only at times of absence or loss.

• • •

LASTING The sibling relationship is probably the longest lasting relationship in our lives. By the time we reach adulthood, or certainly by the time of our aging years, our siblings are the people we have known the longest. We have known them longer than our spouses, even longer than our oldest or dearest friends. They remain the only ones left who can share or confirm our earliest memories and who can protect our pasts from disappearing. Even though our relationships with our siblings may not be the best, the closest, the easiest, or even the most important, they are the most enduring, from the beginning to the end of our lives.

chapter two

CHILDHOOD SIBLINGS: IN THE BEGINNING

In our childhood years, we and our siblings are closer together than at any other time in our lives. We live in the same homes with our parents; we sometimes share the same bedrooms; we usually eat the same foods; we hear the same stories; we are taught the same lessons.

These early relationships with our siblings also bring many important "firsts" into our lives— they are our first peers, our first rivals, our first role models, our first allies, our first enemies. And, for different reasons and in different ways, these firsts last the rest of our lives.

BEFORE THE BEGINNING

It is our parents who make choices about whether to have children, how many to have, and when to have them. Their choices depend on their marital relationship, financial stability, living arrangements, family expectations, and, of course, "accidents" and chance. But basically, the very existence of our siblings, and therefore our relationships with them, is not something that is our choice.

Long before we are born, there are influences developing that will affect us all our lives. The nature of our sibling relationships actually starts with our parents, who are themselves products of their own histories—who they are, what their own sibling relationships were, and what they bring to and expect from their homes and their families. In a sense, we are all products of the past. As children, we reflect our parents' histories just as our own children reflect our histories.

Each generation reacts to its own past, even if unintentionally or unknowingly, and may do so in opposite ways. Some people may seek to recapture, imitate, or perpetuate the past. Others may try to reverse, improve, or escape the past. Our parents may want to create with us, their children, the kind of sibling relationships they wish they had had. Or they may want to reconstruct with us the kind of sibling relationships they recall having had, whether those recollections are accurate or not.

For example, parents who remember the loneliness of being an only child may choose to have

several children to provide the sibling companionship they missed or fantasized about. However, parents who were one of several siblings may remember
the lack of attention or privacy they had and therefore choose to have only one or two children to provide the time or resources they longed for or missed.
Other parents may have enjoyed their childhood sibling relationships—the singularity of being an only
child or the support of being one of several children—and try to replicate this with their children.

In addition, our parents may also have had feelings, even fantasies, about what kind of children they
hoped to have. Certainly, these preferences cannot
affect the reality of what happens, but they can affect
the reactions to that reality. For example, fathers or
mothers may prefer children of their own gender
because they feel they can understand or relate to
them better or will be able to do more with them. Or
they may desire children of the opposite gender to
bring a different perspective to their own experiences
or to avoid making comparisons to themselves.

Parents may want children with certain qualities—children who are compliant and easily grati-
fied, to make child rearing easier; or children who
are active and challenging, to bring the joy of stim-
ulation to the parents' lives. They may want children
who are like themselves in nature and behavior, with
whom they can identify. Or they may prefer in their

children particular personal qualities they feel are lacking in themselves.

In all these different ways, our parents can set the stage for us and our siblings even before we are born. As children, we inherit these scripts that were prepared for us, unintentionally or unconsciously, by our parents.

THE SHAPING FORCES

As children growing up together in our family homes, we find our sibling relationships shaped by a number of other forces as well, which are also beyond our control. We are affected by our individual genetic inheritance and our personal family circumstances, especially such factors as birth order, gender, and temperament. We do not create any of these forces; indeed, in a sense, they create us. They shape who we and our siblings are and how we relate to one another. They shape our relationships with our parents. They also shape the ways we perceive these different relationships.

• • •

BIRTH ORDER Some childhood-development specialists theorize that birth order not only affects a child's family relationships but also affects a child's very personality. According to this theory, firstborns are more conventional, more closely relating to and imitative of their parents, and more socially assertive. Children born later are described as more radical and risk-taking, because they must compete more for parental attention and find new ways to win parental approval.

Whether or not one agrees with this theory, it is clear that birth order does create differences in a child's perspective, treatment, and circumstances. For example, the oldest sibling can enjoy a sense of power and superiority over younger siblings. At the same time, the oldest sibling may resent the feeling of replacement or intrusion that younger siblings can cause. Equally, being assigned responsibility for younger siblings can cause resentment.

Younger siblings, on the other hand, may enjoy special pamperings or privileges but may resent enforced subservience or obedience to older brothers or sisters. They may also feel envious of older siblings' strength, skills, or knowledge and find themselves frustrated as they try, but often fail, to emulate or equal their older siblings.

Middle children may suffer the disadvantages of both positions, often resenting both older and younger siblings and feeling left out or excluded by them. In a sense, each of these birth-order positions brings its own rivalries and its own sensitivities to differential treatment in the family. In addition, the age differences among the siblings can often make their relationships closer or more distant.

Birth order can have an indirect effect on parents' skills and comfort with parenting. First-time parents may be delighted and excited with their brand-new child but also uncertain and apprehensive. Whereas parents of second, third, or later children may be more confident and relaxed about child rearing but also more tired and preoccupied than with the first child.

An odd or even number of siblings in a family can also be a factor. If there is an odd number, say three or five, one child is almost always excluded or left out in some way, although it may not necessarily be the middle child or the same child each time. If there is an even number, say four or six, there are usually alliances of pairs, which may shift from time to time depending on particular circumstances. And if there are only two siblings, they may be intense adversaries or intense allies. Indeed, they are usually both at different times, and this appears to be especially true of two siblings of the same gender—and even more so of sisters.

• • •

GENDER Another force that shapes us as children is gender, which includes our family's views and values about gender. Parents may have certain preferences for sons or daughters because of cultural, religious, social, or economic reasons. Sons may be considered important in order to carry on the family name or business. Daughters may be considered important as family caregivers or maternal assistants. As a result, gender may define children's roles or positions in the family and their relationships with each other. Also, depending on the gender of the earlier children, parents may want later children either of the opposite sex to complement the older ones or of the same sex to be companions for them.

Research has clearly shown that gender can directly affect the bonds among siblings, either positively or negatively. Same-sex siblings more often than not feel closer to each other. Sisters tend to talk to each other more and spend more time with each other. Brothers tend to play with each other more, and their play may be competitive. On the other hand, different-sex siblings, who tend to be more separate from each other, may take on more clearly defined or assigned roles with one another—leader or follower, protector or victim.

It is also clear that parents have different expectations of their sons and daughters, thereby influencing our development as well as our relationships. Parents usually talk more to little daughters, train them more in social skills, and permit them less autonomy. Little sons are usually encouraged to be more independent, more physically active, and less expressive.

We don't know how much these differences are due to nature and how much due to nurture, but we do know that little boys and girls respond to these implicit parental instructions. Children's behaviors become magnified when they play together with their own gender. Little girls tend to behave as they are stereotypically supposed to, and so do little boys. As a result, same-sex siblings are usually kept together more in the home, because they share similar activities and behavior expectations, and because they relate more predictably to one another.

• • •

TEMPERAMENT Still another force shaping our sibling relationships is temperament, including its offshoot: personality. We know that we and our siblings are different as adults, but so were we different as children. Some children are complacent and others combative; some are responsive and others reserved; some are smiling and others serious; some are easy to be with and others stressful. We also know that our temperaments do not seem to develop gradually over time but seem to be a part of us and within us at our birth. Our temperaments were not chosen by us, nor would we necessarily have chosen them if we could. However, they help shape not only our personalities but also our relationships with the most important people in our childhood lives—our parents and our siblings.

Ironically, even if we recognize our siblings as having developed personalities similar to ours, there is no guarantee that this will automatically or easily bring us closer together. We may feel either more comfortable or more competitive with brothers or sisters who are like us. And differences in personality may actually seem complementary rather than conflicting. In other words, our personalities and those of our siblings can bring us together or tear us apart—and probably both at different times.

Our personalities as children can also set the tone for the way our parents raise us. It's not that our parents love us less than they do our siblings, but they do love us differently. A difficult and demanding child may give rise to nervous and anxious parents, just as an easier and more gratifying child may result in relaxed and satisfied parents.

Our sibling relationships are further shaped by our perceptions of what our parents do with each of us and want from each of us. For example, if one sibling is considered to be the "ideal" child or seems to receive most of the visible rewards, we feel envious or angry toward him or her. If competition with that sibling seems hopeless, we may become distanced, and we may reject that sibling. On the other hand, if one sibling seems constantly criticized, corrected, or ignored, we may pity, protect, or sometimes even patronize him or her.

Our parents can unintentionally script us into certain roles, such as the "good" child, the "difficult" child, the "happy" child, the "quiet" child, the "bright" child, and so on. The extent to which we and our siblings do or do not fulfill our parents' expectations affects our relationships with each other as well as with our parents. Actually, as children, we do not really want to be loved equally; we want to be loved unequally, *more* than the others. We fear that the amount of parental love is finite— if our parents also love another child, it means that we will be loved less. Yet, as children, it is our siblings whom we blame, not our parents, for any perceived favoritism. Deep down, we do not want to believe that our parents could love another child more than us; therefore, it must be the fault of the brother or sister.

FIRST ENEMIES, FIRST FRIENDS

There is far more to our childhood sibling relationships than our difficulties, differences, or jealous rivalries over parental love. Our siblings are more than our first enemies; they are also our first friends. Indeed, our childhood development is greatly influenced and assisted by the presence of these other children in our families. We and our siblings do take away from each other, but we also give to each other.

Our siblings are our partners in our first peer relationships. They provide our first experience with others of our own generation, even of our own size, appearance, or position. As such, they become prototypes for our future relationships with other peers who will later become part of our lives—friends, classmates, acquaintances, colleagues, and so on.

With our siblings we have our first experiences relating to others of our own age. We learn how to play with them, get along with them, work with them, even fight with them. We learn how to share toys, resources, activities, and time. We learn how to communicate our wants, needs, and feelings. We learn how to handle disagreements, negotiate differences, and win or lose as positively as possible. We learn how to be competitive but also supportive; loyal and loving but also self-reliant. We learn how to balance our need for intimacy with our need for independence.

We form a special group with our siblings within the family itself, and we experience with them a unique kind of connection. We are each other's flesh and blood, and we know each other and belong to each other in unique ways that no one else can share or duplicate. Though quarrels between us may be

frequent as well as inevitable, they are usually for-
given, forgotten, or overcome through affection or
simply the close proximity of living together. There
is a sense of instant communication and mutual
understanding with one another, as though we share
a special language or private memories. Our siblings
can be allies against parents whenever we, as children, wage our silent, secret, but unavoidable wars
against them. Siblings also assuage feelings of loneliness, which is one of the main reasons an only child
will wish for a brother or sister.

In addition to our parents, our siblings are the
first mirrors of our identities. We learn from them
what we are like. They help us see who we are, and
because they do not carry the same kind of power
over our lives as our parents do, their judgments
about us seem safer and more acceptable. They are
also our first role models at our own peer levels.
They teach us by their example the meaning of
being male or female. They give us lessons that no
one else can about what it means to be a child.

As children, adolescents, and young adults,
we often look for—and, in fact, may even try to
create—ways in which we are different from our
siblings. This is sometimes referred to as de-identification and is part of our need to establish our own
separate individualities. It is not until our later years,
as mature adults or older individuals, that we begin

to look for, rediscover, and actually acknowledge the ways in which we are similar.

. . .

In our childhood years, when we are closest together, we forge our sibling relationships—relationships shaped by our family's histories, our heritages, and our home circumstances. In our adult years, these relationships seem to diminish or even disappear as they become displaced by our separate, adult, independent lives and families. Finally, in our later years, we may begin to give more thought to our siblings as part of the natural process of remembrance and life review. Yet, throughout all these different ages and stages, our sibling relationships persist. Even if our brothers and sisters do not play a prominent part in our lives, they are nevertheless always a part of our lives.

chapter three

ADULT SIBLINGS: THE GREAT DIVIDE

When we become adults, we grow the furthest apart from our siblings physically, personally, and socially. We lead different lives in different homes and in different places, and we do different things with different people.

These changes are the inevitable and necessary steps in our process of emancipation and individuation. Indeed, it is those people who remain unchanged geographically and emotionally in their same early roles and relationships, who seem most unable to grow completely or comfortably into independent adulthood.

Usually the first and most defining step in our progress toward adulthood is leaving our families of origin, because we are not just leaving a physical place but a psychological place as well. For whatever reasons we move out, and to whatever places we move, our relationships with our siblings will never again be the same.

CHANGES THAT SEPARATE

It used to be in other times and other cultures that parents and their adult children all lived near each other, sometimes even with each other, in close-knit arrangements. These kinds of extended families have now become rare. Today, for better or worse, to become an adult means to leave one's original family—along with the roles played there as a child and as a sibling—and to move into new families and new roles.

We leave our parental homes for many possible reasons. It may be that we reached the age of legal adulthood. We may be beginning a new educational or career opportunity in a new place. Maybe we are making a new personal attachment to a significant other. Or perhaps we are marrying and looking forward to having new families and homes of our own. In any case, this move is a milestone in our lives. Whatever the particular reasons or circumstances, it means that we will no longer be living with our siblings in the same family home, and no longer will we be part of each other's daily lives. Except for some possible unusual circumstances, we will probably never again be so close.

When we move out of our family homes, we may also move out of the neighborhood, out of the city, out of the state, even out of the country. Each of us moves where we want or need to be. It can be for financial, career, or educational reasons; for health needs (climate); or for the sake of ourselves, our partners, or our spouses. As a result, our new geographies, as well as our past histories, affect our adult relationships with our siblings.

Research has shown that siblings who are geographically close tend to remain more personally close—they see each other more often, know more about each other, and are more involved in each other's lives. This is not necessarily intentional; it is simply a matter of ease. If we live apart, especially far apart, it requires planning, time, effort, and expense to sustain regular, long-distance contacts. It may seem more than our adult lives and budgets can afford. These obstacles weaken or fragment our emotional connections as we lead lives that have less and less to do with each other.

When we and our siblings establish our own separate adult identities, we become peripheral to each other's lives. We no longer see ourselves primarily as children or siblings in our families of origin but as spouses and parents in our new families. The sibling relationships we care most about are not our own but our children's. Our energy, our efforts, our concerns, and our hopes are now bound up with the people who are the most important in our daily lives. They are the ones whose love and happiness we want, work for, and worry about. It's not that our adult sibling relationships vanish from our lives, but they simply become relegated to the background.

Sometimes having children of our own can bring adult siblings together, at least temporarily, through the common role of being parents. Sometimes, though, it can further separate us because of our new preoccupations and responsibilities. Sometimes our children and our siblings' children may even be used as vehicles for our old rivalries or unresolved issues.

Still another factor affecting our relationships may be the entry into our lives of in-law siblings, especially the siblings of our spouses. We may visit them more if they are closer to us geographically. They may share some of our current circumstances. Often their presence is less complicated or emotionally charged, in which case they may be easier to spend time with than our biological siblings.

As adults, we may follow different lifestyles from our siblings. We may engage in different kinds of social activities, pursue different hobbies or interests, and associate with different friends. We may be limited or liberated by different levels of income or finances. For some of us, we may have been aware even in childhood of personal differences with our siblings, but we lacked the permission or possibility of doing anything about them. But now, in our separate adult lives, we have more opportunities and means. We may actually look for and live out these differences as proof of our independence. Indeed, for some of us, it may actually be a relief to escape from the presence, pressure, or shadow of our siblings and be able to become more ourselves—or whatever selves we think we can or should be.

Adulthood therefore brings various kinds of separations from our siblings, causing both simplification and loss in our relationships. These differences and separations should not necessarily be considered rejections, they are simply a reflection of the personal and circumstantial realities of our lives. Just as we needed to separate physically from our childhood family roles in order to grow up, so, too, do we need to separate emotionally as part of our normal adult development.

For the most part, we probably see our siblings and speak with them as often as events require or as special occasions remind us. And when we do, we probably argue or disagree less than we used to. Our lives may have changed too much by this time to either share much or fight much with each other. Although the details of our childhood squabbles seem to diminish over time, the underlying issues that caused them do not totally disappear. They merely fade into the background because our relationships with our siblings have moved into the background. This probably makes for less overt or explicit stress between us, but it also makes it more difficult and less urgent to deal with any issues between us. As a result, whatever is unresolved will probably remain so. It may become disguised, displaced, or seemingly dismissed, but it will not really be forgotten or finished.

In some extreme situations, adult siblings can become so totally estranged from one another, for reasons they may not even be fully aware of or willing to admit, that they see each other only at required or ritual occasions. One psychologist referred to this as "a family tragedy" and described it as more common than acknowledged. Such estrangement can even extend to the next generation. Not only can we lose our sisters or brothers but also our nephews or nieces. Our own children might never know their aunts, uncles, or cousins.

THE TIES THAT BIND

During this time of our adulthood, probably the strongest link keeping us connected with our siblings is our parents. Depending on their conditions and circumstances, our parents serve either actively or passively as "kin keepers."

• • •

ACTIVE KIN KEEPERS In our early adult years, our parents are still reasonably well and functioning. Generally they are the ones who initiate, encourage, arrange, or even mediate interactions and are at the center of events that bring family members together. They host, plan, and invite children and grandchildren to special family and holiday activities, such as Christmas dinners, Passover seders, or July 4 picnics. Adult children, most often daughters, may help with the preparations, shopping, and cooking, but our parents are the ones who actually preside over these family gatherings.

On these occasions, when we and our siblings are once again together in our parents' homes and presence, old feelings become reignited and old roles reemerge. We tend to see our siblings and ourselves as we did in the past—the bossy big brother, the pesky little sister, the copycat, the show-off, the leader, the follower, and so on—rather than as the adults we have become. Perhaps we do this because those remembered roles are easy and familiar, especially in the parental environment. Perhaps we subtly invite and encourage the roles from one another. Or perhaps we're really just not sure how to behave with each other now that we all have grown up.

Our parents may also try to hold the family

together, perhaps subconsciously, by perpetuating our former roles or behaviors, even though such roles no longer fit. They may still try to negotiate between us, smooth out differences or disagreements, or explain each of us to the other. Sometimes they may even try to tell us how to perceive each other, what to say to each other, how to treat each other, or what to think about each other. It is probably their way of trying to keep their children close and their family strong, almost like a last act of parenting. However, these tactics can no longer work because we are no longer the same children we once were and they are no longer the same parents.

Another way our parents actively keep us connected with our siblings is by keeping us informed about what is happening in each other's lives—graduations, promotions, travels, accomplishments, even problems or illnesses. They remind us about one another's birthdays, anniversaries, and other life events, and urge us to send cards, write letters, and make telephone calls.

These parental efforts can make us feel either closer to our siblings or even further apart. On the one hand, we feel annoyed, resentful, or infantilized by these interventions. On the other hand, we feel secretly pleased by what we learn about our siblings and what we know they will learn about us. Deep down, it seems, we actually want our siblings to know about our lives, especially our accomplishments; and we are surprised at the strength of the interest and pleasure we feel when we know about theirs. It also comes as a surprising realization that as adults we not only still crave and value the approval of our parents but now also that of our siblings.

• • •

PASSIVE KIN KEEPERS There is another scenario that occurs later in our adult years in which our parents become passive kin keepers. This happens when they begin to fail in health, strength, or capacity and begin to need our personal, physical, or financial assistance. Instead of their role being defined by what they are trying to do for us, their children, their role is defined by what we are trying to do for them, our parents.

We begin to feel new connections to our siblings because of our shared concerns and shared efforts for our parents. But each of us, out of our own different needs and circumstances, may propose or desire different solutions. As a result, our parents' illnesses or infirmities can create a reorganization of family roles and relationships. Although all siblings are genuinely concerned, it is usually one particular sibling who takes on the role of primary caregiver—providing direct assistance, making necessary decisions, fulfilling daily needs, even taking the parents into his or her own home and life. Often the oldest sibling, especially the oldest daughter, assumes this responsibility.

Sometimes the role is filled purely voluntarily by one of the siblings, as an act of filial duty; sometimes it may come as a result of explicit or implicit assignment. There may even be a competition for the position of "most dutiful" or "best" child. Or it may be the sibling who is closest geographically, simply out of convenience; the most affluent sibling, the one who can best afford the cost of care; or the sibling who has the fewest other responsibilities, who presumably has the most available time. It may be the sibling who was always seen as the parental "favorite" and is now expected to, or feels the need to, fulfill special responsibilities in repayment. Or it may even be the sibling who sees this as a final opportunity to win parental approval and become, at last, the beloved and indispensable child.

Whatever the reason or combination of reasons, one particular sibling often takes on a different role from the others. She or he becomes the intermediary in the family. All communications with or decisions about the parents must now go through this sibling. The others may make inquiries, offer suggestions, and provide occasional help, but it is clear that this particular sibling, by virtue of being the caregiver, has become central and primary in the relationships among the sisters and brothers.

The noncaregiving siblings, especially those who are geographically distant, often feel both guilty and relieved by these arrangements. They sympathize with their sibling's special burden but are grateful they do not have to bear it themselves. Yet they sometimes feel envy as well for the special and close role it brings. Indeed, when these siblings try to offer suggestions about their parents, as they often do, it may be their only way of feeling helpful or relevant.

When our first parent dies—and these deaths usually begin to occur toward the end of our early adult years—our relationship with our siblings changes again, dramatically even if temporarily. At these times, we feel a strong and immediate sense of closeness with our siblings that we may not have felt for a long time.

We feel newly connected to each other by our shared grief and our common memories of our lost parent. No one else except our siblings can feel the way we do or understand the way we feel, because no one else is also a child to that lost parent. Our spouses, children, closest friends, and other relatives cannot experience the same special pain, because they have not experienced the same special loss—only our siblings have. Even our surviving parent, whose grief may be at a greater depth than ours, may not be able to understand or realize the extent of our own loss.

We feel lonely in our sorrow, and it is only our siblings who can share or assuage that pain. (Indeed, this is one reason why parental death is especially difficult for an only child, even in adulthood.) We find ourselves spending more time with our siblings and together remembering stories and incidents about our lost parent. Sometimes those recollections may differ or be inaccurate, but this doesn't seem to matter. What matters is that we are the only ones who can share whatever memories we have, and this makes each of us feel less alone and our parent less lost to us.

We also feel closer to our siblings as we share questions and concerns about our surviving parent. What will happen now? What should be done? How much longer will he or she be alive and with us? The death of our first parent is a clear warning of the vulnerability of our other parent. It is also a reminder of the mortality of us all.

Yet even while we are struggling together with the pain of our parent's death, some of our old ambiguities and rivalries can rear up. We may even compete with our siblings in our grief over our lost parent or our concern for our surviving one. It's as if we still need to prove to each other, or to ourselves, who is the "better" child. Who misses the dead parent more? Who worries about the living parent more? We may still seem torn by our conflicting desires to be close or similar to our siblings and to be separate or better than them.

Our sorrow and caring are real, but they are also limited by such things as time, our own adult families, and our occupations. It is not that we forget the death of our parent, but our "real" lives back home usually are not basically or lastingly affected. For a time, this experience brings us closer to our siblings as we face this first direct touch of mortality. In time, however, we again separate and return to the different lives we led before.

We are the most distanced from our siblings as adults for reasons that are appropriate and necessary but that may also become negative and painful. It is in the next stage of our lives, in our older years, that we and our siblings again have the opportunity to change our relationships with each other. We have the possibility of choices. We can maintain the distances and differences among us—even passing these on to the next generations of our families—or we can try to rebuild our relationships based on the new realities of our older selves and our present lives. Whichever choice we make, it will probably be our last chance to do so.

part two

Siblings:

the

Lasting

Relationship

chapter four

AGING SIBLINGS: THE LAST CHANCE

As we grow older, we experience changes in ourselves—how we look, how we act, how we feel. We also witness changes in the people in our lives. Our parents begin to fail, our children grow up, our friends become ill, our grandchildren are born. These events change us, and they change the people in our lives. They also change all our relationships with each other.

There are four major life events during our later adulthood that have a special impact on our sibling relationships. Each of these events is an expected part of the normal aging process, so we all go through them. We experience them in different ways, however, and learn from them—or not—in different ways as well.

LOSS OF PARENTS

The first major life event is experiencing the loss of our parents, which carries a powerful emotional impact regardless of how old we are or how old they were. Although there are some individuals whose parents live to a very advanced age, such that "children" in their seventies are taking care of their 90-year-old fathers or mothers, they are a minority. For the majority of us, our parents fail and die, eventually and inevitably, when we are in our fifties or sixties.

During our early adult years, while our parents were still reasonably well, they actively kept the siblings together by acting as kin keepers. When our parents aged or became ill, the siblings remained connected by their common concern or caregiving for them. The death of these parents suddenly removes that central link and brings changes in the relationships among the siblings in different, surprising, and sometimes opposing ways.

Sometimes, without that parental connection holding them together, siblings simply drift apart, especially if they are already geographically apart, as many are. We may speak to each other on special occasions or see each other at special events, but we increasingly lose touch with each other's lives. Our relationships may remain at a kind of uncertain standstill, weakly drifting or sputtering along. The link to our siblings, which was once provided by our parents, requires effort, time, and especially desire to be retained or renewed—and these may no longer be forthcoming.

Sometimes one of the siblings—again, most often the oldest sister—voluntarily takes on a quasi-parental connecting role and becomes the new kin keeper. She becomes the one who tries to maintain communications, acknowledges special events, gives gifts, extends invitations, remembers family stories, and smooths hurt feelings. The rest of the siblings usually readily accept this arrangement. Perhaps it is simply easier, or it relieves feelings of responsibility or guilt. Perhaps it is comfortable and familiar because it retains or reproduces as closely as possible the family configuration we remember. Or perhaps it is a way, without our even realizing it, of keeping our parents and our past still with us.

On the other hand, with our parents now gone, we may finally feel free to relate to our siblings differently. We may no longer feel the need to hide our identities or protect our independence Now that we no longer have to prove ourselves to one another, we can let go of the differences and recognize the similarities instead. It can be a time when siblings face each other *as* themselves and *by* themselves, without the old connecting or filtering presence of their parents—for better or for worse.

RETIREMENT

The second major life event is the ending of our primary parental and work roles. Our children have become adults and probably parents themselves. We and our spouses are retired or retired enough so that we no longer have the same immediate or structured work responsibilities we used to have. We remain parents, of course, but without the same demands on our time and energy as in the past. We remain active and productive as well, but without many of our formerly imposed tasks and agendas.

Assuming that we still have reasonably good health and resources, we can now voluntarily schedule our own activities. We have the time available and the freedom from responsibility to explore and act on our thoughts about certain things or to go to certain places that we could not in our earlier adult years. It means that we can travel farther or more often to see our siblings who live far away or even close by. We can join them in celebrating milestone birthdays, anniversaries, or births of grandchildren. We can be there to help if our siblings are ill, in need, or simply alone.

Now that our children and grandchildren are living their own separate and competent lives, we are more free to think and care about our first families—our families of origin—and about our siblings, who are the only ones left. They are going through similar life changes in their own lives, so they, too, may have more time, thoughts, and feelings about us.

HEALTH CHANGES

The third important life event occurs when we experience changes in our health. A time comes when feeling well means "feeling well enough," and when health care basically means caring about ill health. Sometimes the most frequently scheduled visits on our calendars are not to friends but to doctors! Medical tests or procedures, which once seemed routine, now cause anxiety beforehand and only temporary relief afterward. It is a time when health problems begin, persist, and eventually worsen. It is the start of the irreversible process of our aging.

Even when these health changes are not life threatening, they are life altering. Our older bodies now change, hurt, and fail in different ways and in different places. There are more things that we do less frequently, less well, and less easily. There is a new and increasing sense of vulnerability, which brings with it the first darkening shadows of our mortality.

These changes are happening to our siblings as well. The kid sister, who loved to borrow clothes or listen in on friends' conversations, suffers a mild stroke and needs assistance taking care of her home and herself. The big brother, who used to act so bossy but also helped with homework, has a heart attack and faces bypass surgery. We rush to see them at the hospital or to be by their bedsides, as they do for us, but we know that this health change will have an impact that reaches far beyond this one incident. It will affect the rest of our lives as siblings.

Even if the time we have spent with our siblings has not been often or particularly intimate, we cannot help but be pained by their pain and troubled by their troubles. It has been said that "whatever happens to my brother, something of that happens to me also." So when our siblings fail or grow ill, we feel our own lives lessened as well. We begin to think thoughts and ask questions that we never did or needed to before this. How will we be the next time we see each other? When will the next time be that we see each other? Will there be a next time we see each other? As a result of these health changes, we feel a new sense of urgency in our relationships with our siblings.

LIFE REVIEW

The final major life event is not a physical or tangible one but an inner one. It is what is often called life review, a process in which we revisit and reevaluate our lives. It is a time when we think about the past, not because we want to go back and live in it, but because it can help us to understand the present.

Our children grow up and grow away from us, as they must. We leave and lose our work friends, as we must. Death and distance begin to take other people as well. As our future grows briefer and our world smaller, the important people and relationships from our past loom larger. Consequently, those who still remain in our lives become more precious, and we feel a need to hold on to them as much as possible. This is especially true of our siblings, who are the only ones left from that long ago past. With them, we have someone else who survives and remembers as we do, and so we feel less alone. Of course, longevity in itself does not guarantee sibling reconciliation or intimacy, but it sets the stage and provides the time to make it possible.

The simple diagram below illustrates the stages of our sibling relationships over the years.

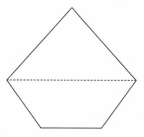

At the top, during childhood, we are close together—living in the same home, with the same family, and under the same circumstances.

In the middle, during adulthood, we move apart

to establish our separate identities, families, homes, and lives. At this stage, we are kept together, either actively or passively, by the surviving presence of our parents. This connection is represented by the broken line in the diagram.

Finally, during our older years, we draw nearer to each other again. We do not, and probably cannot, return to the primary connections that existed during childhood, but we can, and probably do, become closer than we were during our separated adulthood.

There are two things to notice about this stage of our older years. One is the distance that still exists between siblings, which signifies recognition and respect for the different people we have become. The other is the line that now links us, which is not a broken one representing other people's influence but a solid one representing our own direct connections with each other.

The four major life events that change us in our later years—the death of our parents, our work and family retirements, our health conditions, and our life reviews—are all interrelated and part of the aging process. Together they combine to provide the opportunity, the possibility, and the urgency for new and different relationships with our siblings—relationships that are more important than ever because this is our last chance to come together and come to terms.

chapter five

THE SIBLINGS'
STORIES

The following three chapters relate the personal stories of a number of older siblings. Pairs and groups of sisters, pairs and groups of brothers, and pairs and groups of sisters and brothers were interviewed. Given the demographics of the current older population, there were more women than men. All of the people are real, and all of their stories are true. The names and some details have been changed to protect privacy, but without altering basic facts or feelings.

The stories told by these siblings are not necessarily typical of all older siblings, but they do reflect many typical experiences, issues, and behaviors. They also reflect how certain major life events discussed in the preceding chapter affected these particular sibling relationships.

Each of the siblings in the following stories was asked the same two open-ended questions:

1) What was your relationship with your sibling(s) when you were children or young adults? and 2) What is your relationship now? All of the sisters and brothers were encouraged to respond to these questions as freely as they wished.

Sometimes siblings were interviewed together, but more often due to circumstances they were interviewed individually. In a few stories, certain siblings were not available to be interviewed because of health conditions or unknown locations. In these situations, their input could not be presented directly but only indirectly by their siblings. Also, in most of the stories, one sibling tended to be the principal narrator, either because he or she was the most accessible, the most verbal, the most willing, or the most in need of speaking. In only one situation was an elderly parent still living, and that presence still strongly affected the relationship of the two siblings.

The conclusions of these stories can be viewed as neither happy nor sad, good nor bad, right nor wrong. They represent simply whatever relationships these siblings were able to achieve with each other by this stage of their lives. In some situations, there were siblings who wanted to make changes in their relationships but who did not do so because time or circumstance did not seem to allow for it. Or they may have feared taking the risk, feared a lack of response, or feared that change was no longer possible.

In some situations, there were siblings who took small, beginning steps toward a positive change in their relationships—steps that were reciprocated and that felt sufficiently satisfying. The final change they may have been seeking, however, was often not complete—and perhaps never would be. Some siblings would come tantalizingly close to a different and closer relationship, but a particular event, word, or missed opportunity prevented the last, necessary steps. Some siblings felt resignation and regret over the state of their relationships. A few felt satisfied with what they had and simply felt no need or desire for any change.

What is notable in all the stories, regardless of how they concluded, is that all of the sisters and brothers wanted or intended, in some way, to maintain relationships with their siblings, whatever these relationships might be. None of the siblings were willing to accept the absence of any relationship at all, none of them were indifferent to what was happening to their siblings, and none of them felt their siblings were no longer a part of their lives.

Overall, the sisters and brothers in these stories were serious and thoughtful in their responses and were willing to speak and share remembrances about their relationships with each other over the years. The women seemed to talk more readily about their personal feelings toward their siblings, while the men, with some exceptions, seemed more comfortable talking about their activities with their siblings.

In the course of their conversations, certain siblings may have sometimes appeared protective of themselves or of one another. At times some may have engaged in wishful thinking, either intentionally or unintentionally. Others sometimes seemed nostalgic or even naïve. Yet underlying all of their comments was a sense of honest struggle, not only to describe their relationships with their siblings but to try to understand them as well.

THE SISTERS

Chapter 6, "The Sisters," includes the stories of three pairs of sisters, one trio of sisters, and one group of four surviving sisters from an original family of five. These women ranged in age from 68 to 88. There were no brothers in any of these families. (Some of the women could still remember how disappointed their fathers were by the absence of any sons.)

These women were all in reasonably good health, although health changes did play a significant role in two of the stories. In one of those stories, two sisters were still struggling to overcome the remembered impact of long-ago health problems. In the other story, a recent major health change portended a drastic shift in the sisters' relationships.

Overall, the sisters seemed to focus more directly on their relationships with one another than on the impact of parental or familial relationships in their childhood homes. Also, compared with the brothers in the next chapter, the sisters seemed to have been less aware of or less affected by childhood family financial circumstances. Perhaps because they were girls, they had been more protected from work or money problems.

For the most part, the women seemed to try to avoid expressing criticism or casting blame. Even if some blame were implied, it was quickly conditioned by explanations or rationalizations. None of the sisters directly or explicitly expressed strong negative feelings about each other. Even when they recalled disappointments or frustrations, there were more regrets than recriminations. Occasionally, if they could not avoid such feelings of anger, pain, envy, or resentment, they mentioned them only fleetingly and minimized or masked the incidents as minor. At the same time, a few women did make surprising admissions or acknowledge new insights about themselves and their siblings.

THE BROTHERS

In Chapter 7, "The Brothers," two pairs, one trio, and one set of four brothers were interviewed. These men ranged in age from 70 to 84. Among the brothers in these stories, three were not available to be interviewed—one due to a sudden, serious illness; one due to diagnosed dementia; and one because his location was temporarily unknown. This last situation was the only occurrence of a sibling totally separating himself from the others, but this was a temporary arrangement due to his personal lifestyle rather than a purposeful estrangement.

The men's recollections and responses were different from the women's in some interesting and unexpected ways. One probably predictable way, however, was in how the brothers' work roles affected their relationships with each other. Both the kinds of work they had done and the degrees of success they had achieved were factors in how they felt connected to each other.

Another noticeable pattern could be seen in how some brothers' relationships with their fathers strongly influenced, both positively and negatively, their relationships with each other. In these situations the fathers had been strong, demanding, or difficult while the mothers had been rather detached or ineffectual.

One quite unexpected difference was how some of the men actually expressed regret at not having any sisters. The women had recalled only their fathers' regrets but not their own at having no brothers.

Furthermore, the brothers even suggested that, perhaps, if they had had sisters, they might have kept in closer touch with each other over the years.

THE SISTERS AND BROTHERS

The siblings in Chapter 8, "The Sisters and Brothers," consisted of two mixed pairs (an older sister and a younger brother, and an older brother and a younger sister); a trio of two younger sisters and an older brother; and a remaining trio out of six siblings (a younger brother, a younger sister, and the oldest sister). The sisters and brothers ranged in age from 68 to 93.

There were more women than men among these siblings. When siblings were together, the women were usually the major spokespersons. In one situation, a brother was unable to be involved because he was recovering from a recent, severe stroke, and a brother-in-law offered to provide input instead.

Two important patterns could be noted in these stories. First, it was clear from the memories of these sisters and brothers that gender differences played crucial roles, especially in their early sibling relationships. In their later years, this focus was somewhat superceded by health circumstances and distance from one another. In general, these siblings described complicated relationships that were shaped not only by differences in gender, but also by age and family circumstances. In the mixed pairs—one brother and one sister—the sibling relationships seemed particularly intense or stressful. Perhaps the presence of multiple siblings in the other stories offered more possibilities or protections.

The second pattern had to do with health circumstances. Overall, the sisters, no matter what their ages, seemed generally to be in better health—feeling better and functioning better—than the brothers. For all of them, though, health was an ever-present and important concern. The awareness or occurrence of illness as well as death in their families seemed either to bring the siblings closer together in some way or to sharpen their sense of loss about their lack of closeness.

chapter six

THE SISTERS

SISTERS UNDER THE SKIN

Bess and Laura, now 78 and 70, were always different. For starters, they were almost a decade apart in age. When one was a stylish, social teenager, the other was still a chubby child. When one was a young wife and mother, the other was a bookish college student. When one was already a graying grandmother, the other was just approaching middle age.

In addition to these developmental differences, there were other differences as well. They didn't look at all alike. People always said that Bess resembled their father's side of the family and Laura their mother's. Their personalities were different. Bess was the tomboy and Laura the bookworm. The family comment was that Laura had her nose in books, while Bess had her eye on boys!

As young adults, Laura pursued a professional career, while Bess became engaged in social organizations. They married different kinds of men, lived different kinds of lifestyles, and, because of their husbands' work assignments, moved to locations across the continent from each other.

During the sisters' early adulthoods, their parents lived on the East Coast near Bess. Later they moved to the West Coast for the warmer climate and lived near Laura. During those years, whichever one was the long-distance daughter made a few trips a year to visit her parents. As the parents grew older, she tried to assist in the caregiving in whatever ways she could.

After both parents died, the sisters realized that, because they lived so far apart, they would need some new plan or purpose to keep themselves at least in touch, if not together. So they agreed to alternate visits to each other each year and to alternate telephone calls each month. Laura, always the more organized of the two, volunteered to be responsible for reminders.

For several years, the plan worked reasonably well, and the visits went reasonably well. However, Laura remembers that after several days of being constantly together on these visits, and after having exchanged the obligatory news about their children and grandchildren, they began to run out of things to say to each other. So they began to fill up the time when they were together by doing things. When they were in Bess's home, they visited malls and went shopping, and when they were in Laura's home, they went sight-seeing. They also went to movies a lot, where they could be physically together but not have to think of things to talk about.

Just a few years ago, the nature of their visits changed unexpectedly and unintentionally. It was Bess's turn to visit Laura, but when Bess arrived, she complained of a problem with her hip, which made walking difficult and painful. (She would soon need hip replacement surgery.) So Bess requested that they not do too much or go out too much but simply stay put.

As a result, Laura felt that she had to find other things to occupy and entertain them at home. Almost in desperation, she brought out all the family albums, photograph collections, old letters, and birthday cards she could find. "I was just looking for some things for us to do," Laura recalls. "I didn't expect that what I found would do so many things for us!"

As they spent the afternoons together looking at the old pictures and reading the old handwritten notes, they began to reconstruct and rediscover the circumstances and stories that went along with them. Sometimes they could remember clearly, sometimes only vaguely or piecemeal. Sometimes their recollections agreed, sometimes not. Sometimes they were moved to laughter, sometimes almost to tears.

Because Bess was so much older, she could remember and understand more about the past, or at least she insisted that she could. In a big-sister fashion that amused them both, she told stories, explained events, and identified people that Laura had not understood or known about before. They both remember that visit, not just for what they learned from the pictures and letters, but for what they learned from and about each other.

In the course of those afternoons, they began to notice surprising similarities between themselves. They learned they cooked the same kinds of foods using the same recipes inherited from their mother. They found they liked and disliked the same color schemes and clothing styles. They noticed they used similar words, gestures, and even facial expressions to convey certain reactions.

Bess and Laura wondered, both to themselves and to each other, about those resemblances. Did they both learn those ways long ago as children in their parents' home? Had those always been their ways that had simply gone unnoticed until now? Or was it that, when they were together surrounded by souvenirs of the past, they triggered in each other, even if unintentionally or subconsciously, mutual memories and old habits?

One afternoon a neighbor saw them together and, looking from one to the other, remarked, "Well, you two could never deny being sisters!" Laura and Bess were astonished. Was this visible similarity only due to their being two women of like age, size, and style, or was there really a resemblance? If so, when did they begin to look like each other? In a way that neither one could explain or understand, they both felt pleased.

The day after Bess returned home from this visit, Laura called her to find out how she was feeling. Bess was glad that her sister was concerned and jokingly reminded her that it was not really yet her turn to call. Laura simply said, "That doesn't really matter. After all, how many sisters do I have?"

THE PEASANT AND THE PRINCESS

Jenny and Nan are 75 and 70 years old. They look enough alike to be taken for sisters but enough unalike to give different impressions. They both have dark, flashing eyes and thick eyebrows; dark, curly hair turning gray; and square, firm faces. They are strong-featured rather than softly pretty women. Jenny is shorter and more stocky, and dresses casually, almost carelessly. Nan is taller, slimmer, and more stylishly and expensively dressed. Jenny, in her humorous but self-deprecating manner, likes to explain that Nan got the vertical genes while she got the horizontal ones!

Their parents were both New York school teachers who were educated, articulate, and socially active in liberal causes of the 1930s and 1940s, including the Spanish Civil War, the Scottsboro case, and the boycott of Japanese goods. The sisters remember that their home was always filled with people—their parents' students, colleagues, or fellow activists and social crusaders. Jenny remembers the house as being noisy, crowded, and messy, while Nan remembers it as being exciting and colorful.

Growing up in this environment, they inherited or perhaps adopted their parents' liberal and intellectual interests, but in different ways. Jenny became a teacher of disabled children, and Nan became a journalist.

After World War II, Jenny met and married a young research chemist, who spent his lifetime career working in laboratories on special projects. During those years they lived mostly in small, self-enclosed communities on the East Coast, only a few hours from New York, and associated mainly with scientific or academic professional colleagues. Nan, on the other hand, married one of the editors of the newspaper where she worked as a cub reporter. Even after she stopped working to raise her children, she remained involved in newspaper life through her husband's position, activities, and associates. They lived in Manhattan, did a lot of entertaining, attended numerous social events every year, and traveled in connection with the newspaper.

All of them are retired now. Nan and her husband have remained in Manhattan to be near the newspaper world they both enjoy. Jenny and her husband have moved to a small retirement community not far away.

During most of their adult years, the sisters kept in touch with each other at birthdays, anniversaries, and children's graduations, but they didn't really see each other as often as the manageable distance between them might have permitted. Nan and her husband used to stop off for brief visits on their way to or from their travels elsewhere, but the two men had little in common and little to say to each other, so they usually became bored or impatient. When Jenny and her husband visited Manhattan, they found themselves swept up in a swirl of activities, plans, and people that were part of Nan's lifestyle. Jenny describes herself as feeling "overdressed, overweight, and overwhelmed" when she was there. Her husband, at first claiming work problems and then later health problems, had neither the time nor the desire for these visits, so Jenny went several times by herself—but this solution turned out to be equally unsatisfactory. Either she felt guilty about leaving her husband alone, or she felt lonely and alienated in Nan's world. She ruefully describes it as feeling like "a poor peasant in the princess's palace."

The two sisters speak caringly about each other but simultaneously complain about each other. For example, Jenny talks about Nan's life with a combination of pride, envy, and a twinge of disapproval. It's not that it's a lifestyle she even admires or desires. What bothers Jenny is the seeming ease with which her sister has been able to achieve what she wanted. Nan, on the other hand, maintains that she wants her sister to see part of her life and be part of her life. But she also complains that Jenny seems to keep putting herself down, almost as if she wants people to keep building her up!

Although Nan has continued to invite her to visit, Jenny has continued delicately but resolutely to find reasons not to accept the invitations. She may decline because of her husband's poor health, her own arthritis, the weather, or her children's or grandchildren's needs. "I know she means well," Jenny acknowledges, "but somehow it never works out well." Recently, when Nan pointed out to her that this cycle probably meant that they would see each other less and less over time, Jenny's response was, "I know, and I'm sorry, but I guess that's the way it will have to be."

IN SICKNESS AND IN HEALTH

Ruth and Anna are only two years apart in age, 74 and 72, but their appearances and manners make the age difference seem much more. Ruth is gray-haired and heavy-set, almost obese. She moves and speaks slowly and hesitantly. Anna is also graying and has a stocky build, but here the resemblance ends. She is verbal and articulate. She is quick to ask and answer questions, make suggestions, express opinions, and get things done.

Both of them agree that Ruth's health was a problem and a family concern since childhood. She was sickly, or at least sick frequently, with stomach aches, headaches, and insomnia. She was fearful and tearful. Their parents described her as high-strung, and the family pattern, implicit and explicit, was to try not to do anything that would upset her. The doctors—and there were many of them—prescribed vitamins, bland diets, distractions, and patience.

Anna remembers envying her childhood friends who had sisters they could play with rather than have to worry about. On the contrary, Ruth remembers envying her sister, who was strong and certain, who never seemed to get sick or scared. To this day, Ruth feels awed by Anna's quick and quiet competence. Looking back now, she wonders whether consulting a psychiatrist or psychologist—an uncommon course of action in those days—might have helped her. She wonders whether she might have benefited from some of today's medications, such as Prozac or Valium, which were not known or available then.

When Ruth finished high school, she did not go on to college or to work. Instead, she married while still in her teens, a marriage that quickly produced two children and a divorce. Afterward, Ruth and her two little girls returned home to live with her parents.

Neither of the sisters says much about those particular years except that they were difficult. They both remember lots of crowding, lots of crying, lots of noise, lots of laundry, and lots of confusion. Ruth acknowledges that she never could have managed by herself, while Anna adds, "It was hard on all of us."

Shortly after Ruth moved back into her parents' house, Anna married also, partly (she admits now with a smile to soften any sting in her words) to get away from the house and all of its commotion. She had met a college classmate who was stable, kind, and caring and to whom she would remain married for the rest of her life.

After a few years, Anna had her own two children. Then she and her family moved away when her husband accepted a job offer out of state. She left behind her parents and Ruth and her children, who all lived either together or near each other over the years.

Anna visited her relatives regularly, and, in turn, regularly invited them to visit her, but she was usually relieved when they did not accept the invitation.

Anna says that she assumed Ruth was managing well enough over those years, first with her parents' help while they were still able, and then later with her daughters' help when they were grown. "Besides," Anna explains a bit defensively, "I was an involved wife and mother and busy with my own family." She pauses and adds, "I remember I felt guilty sometimes that I wasn't closer or more helpful." Then the defensiveness returns with a touch of anger, "I needed to take care of my children, not my sister!"

Things are different now. Anna's husband is retired, and her children are both married and living on their own. Ruth is feeling stronger and managing better. She lives in her own small apartment, stays in close contact with her married daughters, who are nearby and available, and finds sufficient companionship and social activities at the neighborhood senior center.

Recently, after some urging and much reassurance, Ruth undertook a trip to visit her sister. One of her daughters drove her to the train stop, and Anna met her on arrival. During the visit, Ruth clearly tried to be as undemanding a guest as possible. She also clearly enjoyed Anna's comfortable home and gourmet cooking, and she was delighted to meet her now grown-up nephews and nieces and their families. Just before Ruth left to return home, the two sisters talked tentatively about plans for another visit.

After her sister left, Anna recalls having mixed feelings. She remembers feeling pleased that the visit was not as difficult as she had expected but also feeling relieved that it was over. At the same time, she felt a little guilty and a little sad about her relationship with her sister. Anna acknowledges doing a lot of thinking now about Ruth, not just about this recent visit but about their entire relationship. She sums it up by saying, "I guess I was so busy trying to avoid being my sister's mother that I didn't try enough just to be her sister."

THREE'S A CROWD

Rachel, 74, Belle, 71, and Abby, 68, are easily recognized as sisters. They are attractive, slightly graying brunettes, still with lithe, graceful figures. All three look younger than their years.

Perhaps appropriately, given her name, the middle sister, Belle, was always the beauty of the family, even being featured in modeling jobs as a young girl. She had two brief and tempestuous marriages before she turned 30 and then a third, sometimes volatile, marriage that lasted.

The youngest sister, Abby, was the dramatic one, both professionally and personally. She wanted to be an actress and performed occasionally in small, local theaters. It was there that she met and was briefly married to one of the young actors. Eventually she settled for becoming a high school drama teacher and married one of her colleagues at the school. Her sisters remember, even now, how Abby, as a young girl, always seemed to be emoting through her dramatic words, gestures, and postures.

It's probably no wonder that Belle and Abby fought constantly as children and young girls over clothes, gifts, liberties, restrictions, expectations, and so on. Each one used her own special quality as a weapon during arguments—Belle her beauty, and Abby her dramatics.

Rachel, the oldest sister, was not like the other two. She was not as pretty as Belle nor as provocative as Abby, and she was certainly not as difficult or demanding as either one of them. She was even-tempered, obedient, reliable, easy to please, and dependable. Even her adulthood seemed to reflect this pattern. She had a long, stable career as a nursery school teacher as well as a long, stable marriage.

As Rachel acknowledges, she was the "good girl" of the family. Not only did she try not to give her parents any problems herself, but she also tried to protect them from the problems that her younger sisters presented. She remembers that she always tried to resolve or calm her sisters' quarrels and negotiate their differences. She tried to get them to work harder at school, accept direction more readily, and be less resistant or rebellious. Even today when she speaks about her sisters, she refers to them as "the girls," as she did in the past.

Early on, Rachel knew she was acting as an assistant or surrogate mother figure, but it was a good role for her because she felt so much more grown-up than her sisters. She made life at home generally easier for everyone. Belle and Abby recall with some embarrassment the difficult children and young girls they once were, but they also recall with appreciation the central and calming presence that Rachel was in their lives.

When their parents died, the old roles simply continued, with Rachel now the good mother instead of just the good girl. Even after all three sisters were married and living in separate places, the two younger sisters still often turned to Rachel for help with their adult lives.

But all of this was changed recently by a drastic event—Rachel was diagnosed with breast cancer. She is trying, as has always been her style, to cope without panic or pity, but even with the cancer in remission now, she realizes that the diagnosis will mean many changes in her relationships. "I want to spend my time and energy with my husband, children, and grandchildren," she says. "I can't worry so much about anyone else anymore, not even about the girls."

Belle and Abby, who confess to still thinking of themselves as the girls, were shocked, incredulous, and frightened when they heard the news of Rachel's cancer. They both are still struggling with what to say to her about it—or whether to say anything at all—and what they can do to help her—or if they can help at all. Belle, speaking for both herself and Abby, describes what has happened as totally unreal and says that neither one of them can imagine a future without Rachel being there with and for them.

As for Rachel, she has come to realize something about her relationship with her sisters, which she shared in a thoughtful monologue. "You know, when I was young, I used to think that I was doing it all for them—for the girls or for my parents—that I was making everything good for everyone. Now I'm not so sure. Now I wonder if I was really doing it for myself, so I could be special, too, in my own way, like the girls were both special in their ways. And maybe it wasn't really as good for them as I thought; maybe it was mostly good for me. So now I don't know whether I helped them or I hurt them. I only know I can't be that way anymore."

THE FABULOUS FOURSOME

Dora, Myra, Clara, and Emma are four remaining sisters out of five. Their oldest sister, Ida, died a few years ago. Dora is the baby of the family and is 70. The next sister in age, Myra, is 80. The others are just two years apart—Clara at 82 and Emma at 84. The sisters laughingly refer to themselves as the A team because, whether intentionally or not, their given names all end with the letter *a*.

Dora was an unplanned and unexpected child—what used to be called a change-of-life baby—born when her mother was past 40. Her older sisters, all preteenagers or teenagers by that time, treated her like a shared toy or doll. They dressed her up, played with her, fixed her hair in curls, and wheeled her about in a doll carriage. Each of the older sisters can still recount a fond or funny story about playing with their "real live doll."

Their father died suddenly when Dora was only four years old, leaving their mother with the baby and four other young daughters to raise. She went back to work as an office bookkeeper to support her family, and the big girls took over many of the domestic and parenting tasks. This meant that taking care of Dora was no longer a game but a responsibility, which all the older sisters shared. They bathed her, fed her, watched her, read her bedtime stories, walked her to school, and checked her homework. None of them remembers any major difficulties or instances of serious misbehavior.

Dora herself remembers her childhood years as a time of having five mothers—her four older sisters plus her mother—who took turns caring for her. She acknowledges having been too young to really remember or miss her father and instead remembers being surrounded by mother figures who were always there for her.

Even as the sisters grew up, Dora continued to be the family baby because of the age difference. In fact, she was still a little girl when her sisters were getting married and having children of their own, and she was often treated as though she were part of this younger generation. She confesses today that she enjoyed being babied. The older sisters agree that they babied her for several reasons: they wanted to help their overburdened, widowed mother; they felt sorry for their littlest sister, who had lost her father through sudden death and her mother through exhaustion and unavailability; and it made them feel mature, maternal, grown-up, and powerful.

Myra, the second youngest sister, is the only one who remembers sometimes feeling envious or resentful because she never had an opportunity to be babied herself. She was expected to grow up and become a caregiver like her older sisters. "We all had to be very responsible," she says, "whether we wanted to or not."

Over the years, the sisters remained close to each other, especially in times of crisis. Several years ago, when Dora's son was critically ill and almost died, her sisters were a constant comfort. When two of the older sisters were widowed, the others were close by to keep them company and do thoughtful things to help. And just a few years ago, when their oldest sister, Ida, died, the sisters remember feeling shocked and lost, as if their whole world had suddenly changed. But at least they still had each other, and they could be together to try to keep things as much the same as possible.

Today the four of them live not together but near to each other in the same senior retirement community. They speak to each other or see each other almost daily. Even if they don't see every sister every day, there is always some shared contact or communication among them.

They are all quick to point out that they have other friends as well, because they each have their own different interests. Dora is the businesswoman in the family and still has some part-time work commitments. Myra is the social activist and crusader for causes, especially on behalf of children. Clara is the amateur artist and sculptress. Emma, now the oldest, used to be the best cook and homemaker in the family but is now ill and frequently housebound. Dora has taken over the driving and shopping chores that Emma can no longer do for herself. With the memory of Ida's death still fairly recent, the other sisters worry about Emma, although they do not openly or directly discuss their fears with each other.

The four sisters still marvel about their relationships with each other over all these years. None of them seems to recall any serious quarrels, angers, or upsets among them. "At any rate," Myra comments, "there was nothing important enough to make any difference between us, nothing important enough even to remember." Dora sums it up for herself by saying, "First, as a little girl, they were like four mothers who took care of me. Then, when I was grown up, they were my four best friends to care about me. I really feel lucky!"

chapter seven

THE BROTHERS

THE RIVALS

Marty is 73, and his brother, Joe, is 70. Marty, although the elder, has always been the smaller, slighter, and quieter of the two. Joe has always been the larger, stronger, and louder one. The two brothers trace their physical and behavioral differences to the differences between their parents. Marty was always like his mother, and Joe like his father. These differences mattered more to Marty than to Joe—and still do.

Marty remembers how he used to wish that he were more like his father and that he could have done things the way his father did. What is unspoken in these memories is the implication that his father might have liked him more if they had been more alike. On the other hand, Joe minimizes the importance of the resemblances but, at the same time, acknowledges that somehow, even without intending to or trying to, he always did things just like "Pop" did.

Both of them agree that their father was a powerful presence in their home, even when he wasn't there, which was often. Their father, who worked his way through school as a youngster, began his own small, clothing-manufacturing business as a young man. Expanding it over the years into a large, industrial plant, he employed more than one hundred people who designed, manufactured, and marketed his products. The business, as it was always referred to, was central to the family's financial state and controlled the family's social activities, because the demands of the business always came first.

Their father worked from early in the morning until late in the evening. Even though Marty and Joe didn't see much of him when they were children, his ideas, demands, and expectations were always clear and nonnegotiable. They both can still remember their mother telling them long ago, "Your father says . . . ," "Your father wants . . . ," or "Your father needs . . ."

When the brothers completed their schooling, it was assumed and expected—without any questions or discussions—that they would go to work in the business and eventually take it over. Since Marty was older, he started working there first. He was mainly interested in finance and economics, so he worked in the company office with the bookkeeper and accountant. When Joe came to work there, he was interested in all the other aspects of the business, including purchasing, production, marketing, and sales.

For Joe, the business was a place of pride, as it was for his father. For Marty, however, it meant work that he didn't enjoy and work that he wasn't even sure he wanted. He felt he couldn't leave, because he didn't want to disagree with or disappoint his father. Over the years, Joe began to work increasingly longer hours, taking on the kind of schedule his father always followed, while Marty struggled to resist those pressures and expectations. Marty's wife made it clear that she would not allow herself to become a "widow to the business," as his mother had been. In addition, Marty began to experience minor physical symptoms, such as stomach aches and headaches, and feared he was developing an ulcer.

Marty cannot recall any particular crisis or specific event that finally led him to leave the business, only that it had to happen. He remembers it as one of the most difficult experiences of his life. His father didn't say much. He offered no special words of surprise, protest, regret, or even anger. Marty remembers he felt both relieved and disappointed by that silent acquiescence, and he still wonders what he would have done had his father tried to alter his decision. He's still not sure whether he would have or not.

The relationship between the two brothers changed after that, not intentionally but gradually. With Marty at a new job, the brothers' work schedules were now very different, so they were not available at the same times. Marty remembers feeling a sense of guilt and shame whenever he was with his father and brother, even though neither one directly said anything (or, as Marty adds, "not in so many words") about the situation. In fact, they didn't even ask him about his new job, as though it didn't exist.

When the brothers did see each other, which was usually at family events or in their parents' home, Marty felt more and more like an outsider because Joe and his father constantly talked about the business—what was happening, what was going to happen, what they hoped or feared might happen. Joe insists that neither he nor his father was trying to exclude Marty. "After all," he explains, "the business was Pop's whole life. That's all he wanted to talk about. I was part of it, so we talked about it. What was I supposed to do?"

Their father died a few years later of a sudden heart attack. Fleetingly, and almost with guilt, Marty thought that now, without their father's presence, it might be easier for him and Joe to get along. But there were just too many other changes going on in their lives by that time. Their mother was ill and needed to be taken care of. Joe, who had no sons of his own, was trying to train his son-in-law to work in the business. Marty was considering retiring and moving to a warmer climate. There just didn't seem to be the time or the opportunity to make an effort or pursue a change.

Both brothers still remember one of the last conversations they had shortly before Marty and his wife moved away. It is not clear, though, whether what was said meant the same thing to both of them. Joe told Marty that he was "smart" because he knew how to take it easy and when to let go. As for himself, he said, "They'll probably have to carry me out, like Pop. I envy you," he added, "for knowing how to take care of yourself." Marty replied that he wasn't sure who was really the smart one and which one should do the envying.

THE PRINCE AND THE PAUPER

Mitchell is 78, and Maury is 74. They are both tall, handsome, graying men who appear to be aging well. Mitchell is particularly impressive looking with a kind of regal posture and physical grace that are likely remnants from his long ago professional athletic career. Indeed, he credits that athletic career for being a major shaping influence in his life and also a source of success. He describes, in his rather charming way, how "being a ball player took me from the *playing* field to the *paying* field!"

While Mitchell was attending college and playing basketball for his school team, a professional coach noticed him and invited him to try out for his pro team after graduation. Then, after a few years of playing professional basketball, Mitchell was noticed by the owner of a prestigious private boys school, who invited him to apply for the position of head coach there.

Over time, Mitchell moved from the position of coach to assistant administrator to chief administrator at the same school. Ultimately, by dint of careful saving and planning, he became the owner of the school. The school was very successful, and so was Mitchell, who found himself reasonably wealthy with a fine home, elegant belongings, and a position of status in his community. He sums up his success story by saying, "It all started with using my hands and ended up with using my head."

Maury's story, while satisfactory, is not quite as spectacular. He attended the same local college that Mitchell did but recognized early on that he could not, or would not, compete with his big brother. He knew that he was a good student, but not as good as

Mitchell; he knew that he was a fine athlete, but not as fine as Mitchell; and he knew that he was popular socially, but not as popular as Mitchell.

He decided to pursue a direction at college that was different from his brother's—liberal arts and journalism. He insists that these were genuine interests and not necessarily due to a desire to "escape" from his brother. However, he realized there was little he could do professionally with that kind of training. He was not interested in teaching school, and jobs in journalism were rare except for people with unusual talent, and Maury knew that he was not one of them.

Over the next few years, Maury went through a number of frustrating, dead-end positions. It was at this point that Mitchell approached him about a special opportunity at his private school. The position, which involved working in personnel and public relations, would utilize his liberal arts and journalistic training. Maury held this position for the remainder of his working career.

Maury makes an adamant point that he worked hard, did a good job, and performed an important service for the school during those years. It almost seems as though he still needs to convince others as well as himself. In fact, he insists that he had to work even harder than others to prove to them that his position and his worth did not depend on his relationship with his brother.

Maury tried to keep his personal and professional relationships with Mitchell separate by main-
taining a careful distance and manner at work. One
unanticipated result of this was a distancing in their
personal lives. They came to see less of each other
socially except for special family events they both
attended. Their separation was further reinforced by
the difference in their financial positions. Maury
could not afford the kinds of entertainment and hos-
pitality that his brother could.

Maury remembers that when their parents
retired, Mitchell purchased a condominium for
them in a retirement community. When they began
to suffer serious failing health, Mitchell arranged
and paid for attendant care in their home, which
continued until their deaths. Mitchell did not ask
Maury for any financial contributions to their care,
making the assumption that it might be difficult for
Maury. But neither did he discuss these financial
arrangements or make any issue or public advertise-
ment of what he had done.

Just a few years ago, Mitchell retired. Since he
was still in good health and certainly in good financial health, and since he and his wife liked to travel,
he wanted to enjoy his retirement years while he
could. The ownership and management of the school
were taken over then by his adult son. Maury decided to retire shortly after this, admittedly because he

would have felt uncomfortable continuing in a position where he would be working for his nephew.

The two brothers still see each other on special family occasions, but otherwise they lead very different retirement lives. Mitchell and his wife travel a great deal and keep active with their other personal interests. Maury and his wife tend more to be homebodies and to spend time with their grandchildren.

Looking back at their sibling relationship, Maury concludes, "My brother is really a prince, and I appreciate everything he's done over the years." He pauses and adds a little wistfully, "It's just that sometimes I used to wish he was a little less perfect and I was a little more perfect!"

THEN AND NOW

Simon, Nick, and Avery are three brothers, aged 78, 76, and 70. There is a strong resemblance among them—brown, curly hair that is somewhat thinning and graying; square jaws; regular features; light blue eyes; and warm smiles.

Since having been diagnosed with Alzheimer's disease, Nick has changed the most from how he used to look and from how the other two brothers still look. He has been living in a local, skilled-nursing facility since the rapid deterioration from his condition started three years ago.

Physically, Nick still seems all right except perhaps for the slight tremor in his hands, which may be the beginning of Parkinson's disease, as yet undiagnosed. He has also become much heavier, partly due to a lack of physical activity and partly due to his avid eating habits, since food now seems to be one of the few things he enjoys.

He speaks very little, so his brothers find it hard to tell how much he understands about what is going on around him or what is being said to him. Every once in a while, he utters a brief comment or shows a reaction that seems to be absolutely "on target." The other brothers find these unexpected, unpredictable responses both hopeful and heartbreaking. They become encouraged for the moment but then devastated when it doesn't last.

Simon and Avery visit Nick every Saturday morning. He welcomes their presence with a smile, although they are not certain whether he really knows who they are or perhaps sees them only as people who are familiar in some way. When they visit, they stay for about an hour. They take him for a walk around the grounds and try to talk to him until he becomes either visibly tired or restless. Then the two brothers leave, go out to lunch together, and catch up on personal and family news before going their separate ways.

This is the way things are now, but, of course,

it used to be different among the brothers in the past. Some things were easier, and some were harder. As children, Simon and Nick were almost inseparable. They were close in age and liked to do the same kinds of things. They were strong, active, and physical. They were quick to fight with one another and quick to make up and laugh with one another.

Their father operated a small, neighborhood candy store, and the two boys helped out there after school. They didn't mind because it meant that they could eat some of the goodies in the store and that they had extra time with their father, who enjoyed sports and roughhousing as much as they did.

Before Avery was born, there was another sibling, a little girl who died of meningitis when she was only two years old. This was not something the two boys or their father talked about, even though it hung over the family like a gray fog at the time.

As a result, when Avery was born their mother seemed to want to hold on to him more tightly, to hold him more closely to herself—perhaps to take the place of the little girl she had lost. Simon still remembers how their father objected that *Avery* was a "sissy" name for a boy, and complained that their mother was too protective of him. Over the years, it became clear that Simon and Nick were their father's boys, while Avery was his mother's boy.

As they became adults, Simon and Nick continued to be "jocks" and sports fans. They both also went into the real estate business, particularly sales and development. On the other hand, Avery was the "nerd," and he was protected and prohibited by his mother from playing contact sports. Instead, he became interested in art, attended design school, and began a career in graphic design.

Today Simon is retired, but Avery continues working on a freelance basis. The two men have long teased each other about their career differences. Simon declares to his brother in mock horror, "I still don't understand what kind of work you really do and how you can make a living from it!" Whereupon Avery retorts in similar mock disapproval, "And I can't understand how you could want to make a living from making people buy houses they don't want or really can't afford!"

When Nick was diagnosed with dementia and later placed in the nursing home, Simon visited him regularly, but Avery only rarely. About a year ago, Simon spoke to Avery and suggested—in fact, requested—that he see his brother more frequently. Avery was uncomfortable with this and explained that the visits were depressing and seemed almost pointless because they didn't appear to make any difference to Nick. Simon answered that even if they couldn't be sure of what the visits might mean to Nick, they could be sure of what they might mean to themselves. "It will make a difference to me," Simon told his brother, "and I think it will make a difference to you, too."

That's how their Saturday morning visits to Nick began, and they have continued ever since. It has become a routine that the two brothers maintain and even look forward to because they have a chance to visit with each other as well as visit Nick. Simon speaks for both of them, with Avery nodding silent assent, when he says, "I feel like I lost one brother, but I found the other one."

TWO BY TWO

This family consists of four brothers: Mel, 84, Mike, 82, Jay, 74, and Larry, 72. Their mother suffered several miscarriages during the interval between the two middle brothers. Ever since they can remember, the brothers seemed separated into pairs—the older two and the younger two. That separation has become even more evident in their older years because of a combination of life events and geography.

Mel and Mike have been retired for several years, each one from a small, self-owned business, and they now live near each other in a retirement community. Both of them are recent widowers, still struggling with the adjustment of living alone after so many years of marriage. They are men of few words, and neither one is comfortable discussing his feelings about being alone. Instead, they compare their problems learning how to cook, shop, and keep their apartments clean. They seem to find comfort in these shared experiences.

The third brother, Jay, also retired recently, after a major heart attack. He and his wife moved to the Midwest to live near their only daughter, who helps them and watches over them. She corresponds periodically with her father's two older brothers to keep them informed about Jay's health—which is not good—and his disposition—which is even worse!

Larry, the youngest, has been married and divorced twice. He has held and given up a number of different jobs in places all over the country. At the present time, he is neither married nor employed as far as the two older brothers know. He is presumed to be traveling, although they don't know exactly where he is. From time to time, he calls them to find out how they are and to reassure them that he is well, but they're unable to contact him in return.

Dissimilarities between the two pairs of brothers stem not only from the difference in their ages but also from the difference in their treatments and expectations in their early years. Mel and Mike are in agreement about this as they talk about their memories of their father as the central and over-whelming figure in their childhood. They remember him as a difficult and demanding man who terror-ized his children and his wife. His wife was fright-ened into silence by his complaints and rages, and his sons were frightened into obedience by his frequent physical punishments.

The two older sons usually suffered their pun-ishments together and would later console each other over them. When they grew older and bigger, they learned how to escape or avoid some of the punishments. It became almost a game of skill for them to know when to hide, when to make up excuses, and how to sense their father's moods. They also learned how to help protect their two younger brothers from their father's wrath through warnings, advice, and interventions.

Mel says, "We helped make it easier for them with the old man. And that was okay because we'd been there and knew what to do. We didn't mind because it made us feel good, almost like we were getting back at the old man in a way."

Another dissimilarity they remember between the two pairs was in regard to the family's financial circumstances. During the Depression, when times were hard and money was scarce, Mel and Mike were teenagers. Their father was a mechanic, but there weren't many job opportunities for him. The two older sons had to leave school when each one turned 14 so he could try to get any job possible to earn money to help the family. They both admit they weren't great students anyway, so they didn't mind leaving school early. It wasn't until many years later, when they were adults, that they began to wonder about what they might have missed.

By the time the two younger brothers, Jay and Larry, reached their teens, World War II had begun, and there were jobs for men with mechanical skills and experience. As a result, money was no longer a major problem, so neither of the younger sons had to go to work at such an early age. Jay finished high school, and Larry even finished college. Both of them went on to jobs and distant places of their own.

Their father died of a sudden heart attack while still in his fifties. All of the sons were out of the home by then and were either married or on their own. By the time their father died, he was no longer the awesome, fearsome figure of their childhood. They felt his absence, but they did not mourn for him.

Mel and Mike both say that their two younger brothers had things "a lot easier" than they did, but they don't express any bitterness or resentment about it. "That's the way things were. In fact," Mike comments, "with all their fancy education and easier bringing up, they don't have any better lives than we do. We always worked hard, we earned enough, and we were satisfied with what we had."

Mel expresses more regret about his younger brothers. "I wish Larry would settle down somewhere or come out here for a visit so we could see him. I wish I could make a trip to see Jay, but I know I can't travel anymore [because of my diabetes and poor eyesight]. I worry about them, and I don't know how I'll ever be able to see them. You know," he adds, "when my wife was here, we all kept in touch more. We were closer. Women know how to do that more than men. It's too bad."

chapter eight

THE SISTERS
AND BROTHERS

MOTHER'S PET

Raye and her brother, Donnie, at 71 and 70 respectively, are only 15 months apart in age. Yet for Raye, that age difference has seemed sometimes much more and sometimes much less than it actually is, especially when they were children.

Donnie's birth was what was delicately called "an accident," because it was not planned, desired, or expected so soon after Raye was born. He was a much desired son, however, and also a large, happy, beautiful baby, which made up for the inconvenience of his unplanned birth.

For Raye their age difference as children seemed more than it actually was because she was always expected to act like the big sister—to be more grown up, well behaved, self-controlled, and responsible than her younger brother. She was also expected to watch over him, help take care of him, monitor him, and, if necessary, protect him.

The age difference between them seemed much less because Donnie was quick, bright, and precocious at a very young age. He walked and talked early. He learned new things quickly and easily. He imitated Raye in what she said and did and was soon speaking as well as and as much as she did—in fact, sometimes strangers thought they must be twins!

Donnie charmed people with his smile and sunny disposition. He was especially adept at making their mother laugh and winning his way out of predicaments or misbehaviors through little jokes or displays of affection.

Though he was extremely intelligent, Donnie was an indifferent student at school. He got into petty mischief and had unpredictable, though not serious, behavioral problems. Raye, on the other hand, behaved as she was expected to in school. She was conscientious and attentive, earning consistently good grades. She went through college dutifully and satisfactorily, whereas Donnie graduated from college only after changing courses, changing majors, and changing schools.

These patterns continued into their adulthood.

Raye married and was a devoted, helpful wife and a caring mother. Donnie married also, but both his marriage and his work life were volatile. There were occasions—kept private and almost secret—when their parents had to provide temporary financial assistance for his legal, business, or personal problems.

Raye was a dutiful and attentive daughter. She visited her aging parents regularly and frequently. After their father died, she made certain to call her mother, who is now 92, every day. Donnie visited his parents only when he wanted to and never on a regular or preplanned basis. When he came, he always brought flowers, candy, or cake. Their mother continues to call him Donnie, not Don, as if he were still the same charming, mischievous little boy he had been, rather than a serious, grown-up adult. Raye comments that their mother still babies Donnie in other ways as well.

Their mother is quite frail now and has recently moved into an assisted-living facility. Her needs are provided for, and she has companionship and supervision. Raye feels guilty about not being able to take her mother into her own home to take care of her. To compensate, she made all the arrangements. She selected the facility, disposed of her mother's excess belongings, supervised the move, and contracted for medical care. She visits her mother frequently, calls almost daily, and consults regularly with the caregivers to assure herself that her mother's needs are being met. Donnie continues to visit only occasionally and at irregular intervals, with Raye phoning him to keep him informed.

In one conversation when the two were together, Raye admonished her brother. "You ought to go see Mama more often. She always asks about you, about when you're going to visit." She adds softly, "Mama always wants to know about you first, even before she wants to know about me or my family."

Donnie tried to defend himself. "I know you think I don't do enough for Mama, but I do what I can. Maybe I don't do the things you do, but when I see her, I make her laugh, I make her happy. I know you don't think that's much, but it's what I do for her."

That was the closest they had ever come to quarreling openly. Raye tends to keep her distress and unhappiness to herself, not expressing her true feelings through words even though she clearly feels hurt. Donnie tends to ignore unpleasantries and turns to other distractions or diversions. After that particular conversation, Raye remained visibly upset, but it was not until Donnie had left the room that she began shaking her head and saying, "It isn't fair. I always try hard. I always do the best I can. It just isn't fair!"

BIG BROTHER

Lily is 81, and her big brother, Ben, is 93. Ben could not be interviewed because he was still recovering from a serious stroke. The information and recollections come from Lily and Charley, her husband of almost sixty years.

The great age difference between these two siblings was due to their parents' protracted separation during World War I. Their father had emigrated from Europe to the United States in 1914, leaving his wife and little son behind, intending to send for them as soon as possible. The war intervened, and the family was not reunited until after it had ended. Lily was born a year afterward.

Lily remembers that her big brother always seemed more of a father figure than a sibling. It was partly due to the age difference, but he was also tall and imposing and seemed to tower over her and even over their parents. He was more educated and sophisticated than their parents, excelling in college, writing for local magazines, giving lectures in neighborhood schools, and dabbling in politics. He had a strong voice and strong opinions, and he exuded an air of command and certitude. So as a child and young girl, Lily always looked up to Ben, literally and figuratively. She even remembers (laughing about it now) how she would polish his shoes for him to show her devotion.

Lily admired and adored her big brother, but she was also a little afraid of him because she worried about pleasing him and meeting his expectations. He had a way, without even raising his voice, of simply making a comment or asking a question that could totally change her mind or behavior. "Is this really the best you could have done on the exam? Is this really the kind of friend you want to associate with? Is this really the impression you want to make on people?"

Lily also remembers the other side of Ben that didn't intimidate her but protected and assisted her. In school, the other children wouldn't dare tease or harass her because they knew about her big brother. He was also the one who patiently and willingly tutored her in math and science. She admits, "I never could have passed those exams without him."

When Lily and Charley met and then decided to marry, Ben's disapproval was clear and unrelenting. On this subject Charley has strong, unforgotten feelings. "Ben never thought I was good enough. I wasn't educated enough. I wasn't successful enough. I wasn't rich enough. I wasn't important enough. And he never changed his mind, and he never let me forget it!" Lily tries to placate her husband, but it is clear that this is a subject the two have discussed and disputed many times before.

Over the many years that followed, the two

brothers-in-law had a polite but minimal relationship. Lily and Ben saw each other only infrequently, but Lily continued to call her brother to tell him about herself and her family's doings. She acknowledges that it was probably not merely to inform him but also partly to seek his approval, just as she had done as a little girl.

As time passed and Ben moved into his eighties, Lily began to see physical changes in him. The once towering figure was smaller; the once imperious manner was hesitant; the once certain voice was slower. Whenever she remarked on these changes, Charley would tell her, "You have to remember how old he is. We're all changing. We're all getting older. And he's the oldest of us all."

A few years ago Ben suffered a series of minor strokes (known as TIAs or transient ischemic attacks), and recently he suffered a major stroke, which left him confined to a wheelchair and in need of full-time attendant care. His right side is partially paralyzed, including his face. One eyelid droops as if he is only half awake, and his speech is sometimes indistinct and hard to understand. His mind is clear, however, even if his speech is not. He is demanding and complaining, railing about his care, his condition, and his fate. He is especially irritable and critical toward the attendant on whom he is now so totally dependent.

Since the stroke, Lily has tried to visit him frequently, but the visits are becoming briefer and more difficult. There is little she can do for him, little she can understand of what he says, and less and less she can say to him. Charley rarely accompanies her on these visits, but he always tries to console her about them. "I know it must be hard for you to see him this way, and I'm sorry," he tells her. "For me," he adds, "I can't be a hypocrite and pretend I like him now just because I feel sorry for him."

Thinking about what has happened to her big brother, Lily has both reflections and regrets. "When I was little, I really couldn't talk to him because he seemed so far above me. When I grew up, we really didn't talk to each other because we had drifted so far apart. Now he's too far gone to really talk to." There is a long, quiet moment before she continues. "I only wish that somehow, sometime, in all those years, there could have been something different between us."

ALL'S WELL THAT ENDS WELL— IN A WAY

Elliot, 79, Lois, 73, and Emily, 71, are a trio of siblings who seem to represent a classic case of middle-child syndrome, in which the middle child feels left out or left behind by both the older and younger siblings. In this particular family, the situation has become further exacerbated over the years because of their personalities and the distances between them. Yet when the three siblings are together, their relationship is evident to all who see them. Physical and behavioral resemblances are apparent in their deep-set eyes, finely sculpted features, certain mannerisms, and similar use of words and gestures.

Elliot, the oldest, was a bright, active, assertive little boy. He was the sole subject of his parents' pride and attention until he was six years old, when his first sister, Lois, was born. He insists that he felt pleased when his parents' supervision focused on her instead, allowing him more freedom and independence.

Lois was a sweet, shy child, and her parents, especially her mother, were delighted to have this little girl, who was so gentle and affectionate and who could be so prettily dressed up and shown off to admiring friends and relatives. But Lois enjoyed this special spotlight for only a brief period of time. When she was two years old, her younger sister, Emily, was born. Emily was also a bright and pretty little girl, but far more outgoing, verbal, and active than her older sister. Indeed, whenever the two girls were together, it was clear that Emily captured immediate attention and admiration. She eagerly and willingly performed for audiences. She recited little poems, sang little songs, and responded smilingly to guests. She was often referred to as "the sparkler" by those who saw her.

As children, and later as young adults, Elliot and Emily especially enjoyed each other's company despite their eight-year age difference. They appreciated each other's bantering sense of humor, they shared strongly felt opinions, and they exhibited driving ambitions. Lois, who was timid and quiet, felt uncomfortable and excluded and clung instead to her mother's consoling presence. Even today, she explains, "I think Mother was protective of me because she worried that I felt left out."

Over the years, the three siblings grew up, married, raised their families, followed their careers, pursued their various interests, and lived in different places. Elliot was involved in computer work and moved to the West Coast's Silicon Valley to become part of the high-tech industry. Lois stayed on the East Coast and married a young man in dental school. She worked with him to develop his professional practice and later became a conscientious mother and a volunteer in community organizations. Emily became an attorney, meeting her husband while both of them were attending law school. After receiving their law degrees, they moved to California, where they set up shared offices but had separate legal practices. When the parents retired, they, too, moved out to the West Coast Sunbelt for the warmer climate.

Lois found herself separated from the rest of

her family, now 3000 miles away. She visited her parents several times a year, even though this was costly and inconvenient for her. She visited even more often after her mother became widowed. She was concerned about her mother's health and living conditions, since she viewed her siblings as too preoccupied with their work lives to provide the time and care called for.

Lois first tried making discreet and gentle suggestions, then more direct and explicit requests, and finally criticisms and complaints. "You need to see Mother more often. You need to spend more time with her. Is she taking her medication? Is she eating properly? Does she have people to talk to? Does she know what to do in case of an emergency? You know," Lois said at last, "Mother really shouldn't be living by herself. She should be with her family." Elliot and Emily remember hearing this and thinking, but not saying, that it was easy to give instructions when you didn't have to carry them out, and that it was easy to be so "good" from so far away.

Not long after, Lois informed her sister and brother on one of her visits that she had decided to take their mother, who was now 90, back east to live with her. She remembers telling them, "No one else could do it, so I felt I had to." The new living arrangement lasted less than a year, during which time their mother's health gradually and perceptibly worsened. Elliot and Emily took turns traveling to visit their mother every few months, with all appointments and information arranged or obtained through Lois. Finally their mother had to be placed in a nursing home, where she died shortly thereafter. Lois brought her mother's body back to the West Coast for burial and then returned to her own home immediately. She did not remain for any family bereavement rituals.

During the next few years, contact between Lois and her two siblings diminished and virtually ceased all together. Elliot and Emily called Lois, usually to find their calls unreturned or their actual conversations brief and uncommunicative. Birthdays and anniversaries went unacknowledged; important events and information weren't shared—even though changes were happening in all of their lives. For instance, Elliot had retired and moved to a senior community. Emily was suffering from severe rheumatoid arthritis, which was becoming painful and crippling. And Lois had several grandchildren who were quickly growing up. Their mother's death had apparently severed whatever ties, however tenuous, that had previously connected them.

Two years ago, something else happened. Lois's oldest daughter, now a mature adult with teenage children of her own, contacted her aunt and uncle to invite them to their grandniece's graduation. She also told them that she thought her mother really wanted to try to reconnect with them but didn't know how. She suggested that perhaps this might be a safe and neutral way to start.

Although Elliot was recovering from successful bypass surgery, and Emily was trying to cope with her physical limitations caused by the arthritis, they accepted the invitation and made the trip to attend the graduation. When the three aging siblings at last met again, it was awkward and uncomfortable, and their conversations were trite and polite. But after a while, they began to share information about their health, their homes, their children, and their grandchildren. Slowly it became easier to talk to one another.

Since then, all three of them have been calling each other more regularly, especially on birthdays, anniversaries, and special, milestone events. They talk about Elliot's upcoming eightieth birthday and how astonishingly fast time has passed. They talk about Emily's worsening health and how ironic it is that "the sparkler" of the family should be the one in the most pain and in the most impaired condition. And they talk about Lois's grandchildren and her frequent baby-sitting responsibilities for them.

Seemingly by unspoken and mutual consent, they do not talk about the several years of silence and distance that existed among them. They do not talk about whatever pain, anger, or hurt they may have felt toward one another. They carefully seem to avoid the past and focus their conversations on the present or immediate future. Touching briefly on what happened, Lois reflected, "There's no point in rehashing what's over and done with. We'll probably never really know who was right and who was wrong." "It's good that we're closer again," Emily comments. Elliot, who is now the patriarch of the family, adds, "I think our parents would be pleased."

ONCE THERE WERE SIX

Once there were six siblings in this family—Edie, Sam, May, Connie, Ginny, and Jerry. Now there are only three left—Edie, the oldest, who is 86; and Ginny and Jerry, the two youngest, who are 70 and 68. The other three siblings died within the past five years, one shortly after the other. Sam died after repeated heart problems, treatments, and surgeries. May died after losing her battle with breast cancer. And Connie died after a sudden, massive heart attack.

When the three remaining siblings are together, certain similarities and differences among them are easy to see. There is a strong physical resemblance between Edie and Ginny. Indeed, Ginny looks like a younger, thinner, darker-haired version of her older sister. Ginny is more quiet, though, more nervous, and more depressed looking. Jerry, on the other hand, doesn't resemble his sister Edie in looks but seems to share her charm, sense of humor, and verbal ease. When they are all together, Edie and Jerry do most of the talking, while Ginny listens intently, nods her head, and seems to concur with what the others are saying.

The three siblings have both similar and differing recollections of their childhood, but they all agree that their household was warm, busy, and often chaotic. This was partly due to the number of children and the age differences among them. "There were the 'big three' and the 'little three'," Jerry remembers, "and for us younger ones, it was like two different generations." In fact, when Jerry first entered school, Edie was already married with young children of her own. His big brother, Sam, the only other boy in the family, was so much older and bigger that they could never play or do "boy things" together.

Ginny remembers that she tried to be close to her nearest sister, Connie, who only wanted to be with or be like her two older sisters. Edie acknowledges that she, Sam, and May did feel especially close. With a sad smile, she adds, "Connie always wanted to be with the bigger kids, but we wouldn't let her. Now she finally is with them by dying like they did."

Growing up, they all remember their father as

having intermittently poor health. They knew that their father was sickly, but they were never told exactly what the health problem was except for something vague having to do with his heart. As a result, their mother was often preoccupied with his care, and the children were expected to care for themselves and for each other. Their mother was always there for them as the ultimate referee or authority, but, for the most part, the children were on their own. "That meant we were all close," explains Jerry, "but not really close. We were close because we would certainly help each other if we needed to, but we weren't close because we were all doing our own thing—not in any bad way, but that's just the way the family was."

Another childhood memory they all share has to do with family finances. Because of their father's poor health, he wasn't always able to work, so the admonition "we can't afford it now" was a familiar refrain. It wasn't that they were seriously deprived in material ways, but they all had to be careful and responsible.

Edie and May, as the two oldest girls in the family, had mothers' helpers jobs to earn extra money. Sam, the oldest boy, had a paper route. Edie still tells stories about those early wage-earning experiences, but she does so humorously as if her memory has transformed them into childhood adventures. The three younger children were more protected from financial problems and responsibilities, though Connie always wanted to work to earn some money like her big sisters, but she was not permitted.

All of the siblings except Edie lived their lives in the same Midwestern community in which they had grown up. Edie left the family home when she got married, was then widowed at a young age, and later moved to be near her children, who had grown up and moved elsewhere. Every year since then, Edie has made a trip back "home" for a family reunion with her siblings and their families. Three of those trips in the past few years, she reflects, have been to attend her siblings' funerals.

Edie, who is generally upbeat and even wise-cracking, becomes somber and reflective when asked which one of her siblings' deaths was the hardest for her. "They were all hard in different ways," she says. "I felt the closest to Sam and May because we were the closest in age, but I knew they both had serious health problems, so it wasn't so much of a shock. With Connie, we weren't as close because there was a bigger age difference—I always considered her one of the younger kids. But her death was so sudden; it was more of a shock.

"They were all hard," she says softly, "but do you know what was the hardest thing of all?" She goes on to answer her own question. "It was the feeling that it was wrong, that I was the oldest, so I should have gone first. But then three of them in a row—younger than me—died instead. And every time, I felt like it was a mistake, like it really should have been me!"

Edie herself is now beginning to experience some cardiac problems, which seem to run in the family. The doctor has advised her against any further major travels and has prescribed medication, caution, and care, but Edie insists that caution and care were never part of her lifestyle. She tries to deal with what's happening with her usual combination of pragmatism and humor. "My heart doesn't seem to be doing what it's supposed to. Well, I guess after all these years, it's entitled to get tired."

Now that Edie can't travel (Ginny and Jerry carefully avoid adding *anymore* to the end of the sentence, as if the situation is only temporary), her siblings have promised to come to visit her more regularly and frequently. Edie reassures them, "You're not going to get rid of me so fast. It certainly hasn't happened so far!" They all join in the joke, saying that Edie is such a tough cookie that she'll be around for a long time. They try to adopt Edie's light and bantering tone, but it doesn't come as easily for them. Jerry turns suddenly serious and says, "Somehow, I always thought we'd all just go on the way we were. It's hard to believe that we all won't ever be together again."

chapter nine

FINDING OUR SIBLINGS, LOSING OUR SIBLINGS

As siblings during this last part of our lives, we are faced with two final challenges in our relationships with each other—finding our siblings and losing our siblings. The first challenge is within our choice and within our control; the second is not.

Finding our siblings means reconnecting with them in new roles and in realistic ways. It is a personal and voluntary process that does not occur automatically. It requires motivation, which we must experience; opportunity, which we must take advantage of; and effort, which we must expend.

Losing our siblings means losing them to illness or death—a happening that is beyond our control. We can only control the ways in which we cope with what happens. In this stage of our lives, death—including the deaths of our siblings—is inevitable and unavoidable. Indeed, the only way not to experience a sibling's death is either to not have any siblings or to die first yourself!

These two final processes, finding and losing our siblings, are not as totally opposite or unrelated as they might at first appear. If we are able to find some satisfying reconnection with our siblings, then the pain of our eventual loss may actually be more bearable. At the very least, there will not be feelings of lost opportunities. There will be grief but not regret.

FINDING OUR SIBLINGS

Some of us may have been able to maintain close relationships with our siblings throughout our lives even though we have moved on from childhood to adulthood and have developed separate lives. However, for many of us, that separation from our siblings carries a physical, psychological, or emotional distance that may be hard to bridge. It is only when we are approaching the end of our lives that we can seriously turn to the task of rebuilding ties with our siblings.

• • •

MOTIVATION The motivation for finding our siblings emerges from some of the changes referred to earlier as part of our aging experiences. One of these changes has to do with our conflicting sense of time. On the one hand, we know we have more time in our days, because we are retired from full-time parenting or work responsibilities. We have more time available to see our siblings, to be with them, and to think about them. On the other hand, we also know we have less time in our lives, as the years seem to pass more quickly and mortality seems to approach more closely. We begin to view the time remaining for us, and the people remaining with us, with a new sense of value and urgency. Therefore, things, people, and circumstances that were taken for granted before, when we thought we had unlimited time, now evoke more attention and more emotion.

Another source of motivation is the understanding that comes from aging itself and from the memories of the important people and events in our lives. As we review our lives' journeys from their beginnings until now, we cannot help but recall those people who were part of our lives and those who touched and taught us in different ways along the path.

With our parents' generation now gone, our siblings are the last survivors and the last reminders of our histories. Their places in our memories and their roles in our lives loom larger than ever before. We wonder as we never did before about our relationships with them. We begin to ask ourselves questions about them. How important is it to us to maintain our sibling relationships now? Are we satisfied with and not merely accustomed or resigned to the relationships we have with them? What do we wish the relationships would be, not in fantasy but in fact? Given our histories and our geographies, are there realistic ways in which we, our siblings, or our circumstances could change to make some of those wishes come true? What would be required of ourselves and of them?

Clearly there are no simple or correct answers to any of these questions. For each of us there are only our own answers, arising from our different pasts and leading to our different futures. Before we can answer these questions about our possible future sibling relationships, we have to try to understand our past relationships—which means trying to understand ourselves as well as our siblings.

In the past, all of us surely have experienced differences and problems with our siblings that may still be remembered but not be resolved. Yet today, we and our siblings are no longer the same people we were in the past. We are no longer each other's enemies, rivals, or victims—if we ever really were. We cannot undo or redo what once may have been. We cannot "even the score" for problems or circumstances that have long since changed or disappeared. To continue to think in these terms, to try to seek some kind of accounting, will only trap us in a past that does not exist anymore and that will shut us out of a future that can exist. Instead of correction or resolution, we need to think in terms of reconciliation—to focus not on the differences that separate us but on the ties that connect us.

We have to let go of certain things yet hold on to others. We have to let go of the fantasies of the ideal sibling we wanted—someone who was always like us and who always liked us. We have to let go of the memories of past pain, anger, or disappointments in each other and with each other. We must instead hold on to and accept what each of us is now—the real and available individuals we have become, the kind of siblings we can and want to actually be to each other. All of us, our siblings and ourselves, are flawed, needy, and imperfect creatures, but in learning to come to terms with our siblings, we will also learn to come to terms with ourselves.

• • •

OPPORTUNITY The second step in finding our siblings is finding the opportunity. There are many different events and occasions that can serve as opportunities to reach out to our siblings, that can serve as keys to unlock or open wider the doors between us.

There may be anniversaries of special times from our family histories or childhood memories that have been forgotten or overlooked in the rush of passing time. Now we can recall them and remind each other of them. We can reminisce about trips we took together as children with our parents; about a special family ritual, routine, or holiday observance; about a particular adventure or misadventure that we can laugh or even cry about now; and so on.

There may be special current events that invite our attendance or attention, such as children's or grandchildren's births, graduations, or weddings. Certain milestone events occur during our senior years—70th, 75th, or 80th birthdays as well as golden anniversaries—that offer opportunities for participation and celebration.

Negative milestone events, such as illnesses, hospitalizations, and operations, can bring siblings together, too, through our shared worries and fears. Family problems with children or grandchildren—divorces, failures, financial losses—can trigger our concern and require our assistance.

Each of these opportunities can provide a shared experience and can focus our attention on each other, even if only temporarily. Each opportunity can build a bridge, however tenuous, that can begin to span the distances and differences among us. Each opportunity can be a chance for closeness—if we choose it and use it.

• • •

EFFORT Effort is essential to bring about whatever changes in our relationships we want now. Do we decide to take the initiative ourselves, or do we wait for our siblings to do so? Do we take the initial step the first moment we wish to or care to, or do we wait for some safe, special, or inviting occasion to come along? How much, how hard, or how often do we want to try? How much or how little do we expect in response?

On a practical level, can we see each other more often, more regularly, or more frequently? If we live far apart geographically, can we make trips to visit each other or take vacation stops along the way to see each other? If we live close to one another, can we do more things together—attend the theater, go out to restaurants, or visit local sites? Can we get together to celebrate holidays or each other's special events? Can we simply keep in touch and keep each other informed?

On a personal level, can we or do we want to tell each other about our inner lives and innermost feelings? Can we share intimate problems and concerns, or can we listen to theirs? Can we ask for or expect help or advice from each other—even though we probably hope none of us will really need it?

It takes only one sibling to make the first step, whatever it may be. It can be a telephone call, a birthday card, a visit, an invitation, a gift, or a conversation. It is comforting, though not surprising, to know that most often there will be relief and response in return. This outreach does not have to (and probably will not) bring instant accord or immediate intimacy. It may feel limited or awkward, especially at first, but it can (and probably will) bring something that eases and pleases into the relationship.

After all, our siblings are facing the same imperatives of the aging process that we are, and all of us know that we have less time left in our lives. During that time, we are seeking something different and something more—not *from* them but *with* them. We may not even know what *more* may mean—for them or for us.

Closeness between siblings does not have to deny the existence of our differences, but neither do our differences have to preclude the existence of a closeness. There is also no one state of closeness that is ideal or that is possible for all. Although it is certainly too late for all the things between us to change, it is perhaps not too late for some things—enough things—to change. We may still wish that things could have been different, but we no longer try to change what we realize is unchangeable. We now look for what is possible and not for what is necessarily perfect. A new or different relationship with our siblings may be less than what we once may have wanted, but it will be more than what we have now.

A final thing to remember is that the ways in which we find our siblings during this stage of our lives sends an important message to our children who have siblings. We serve as role models for them as they grow older with each other.

LOSING OUR SIBLINGS

Death is no longer a stranger to us by this stage of our lives. We have experienced the deaths of our parents and most other members of their generation. But whenever a death occurs, no matter how old the person was or how old we are, it is a profound and irreparable loss. These losses change the roles and relationships in our lives. Yet they are also expected and inevitable, and they are a part of the natural order of things. They bring us sorrow but not surprise.

We are now also beginning to experience the serious illnesses and even deaths of our peers. No matter how often or how expected their deaths may be, each one is new and each one is hard. We are never really ready or prepared for them.

The deaths of our siblings also bring major loss and change to our lives, but for different reasons and in different ways. Somehow siblings' deaths are viewed with less significance, sympathy, and serious attention than parents' deaths, and we receive fewer supports and condolences. Perhaps because our lives seem to continue so apparently unchanged on the outside, there is less awareness of any pain or loss we feel on the inside. Perhaps because we may still have other siblings, the loss is not considered to be as unique or irreplaceable. Perhaps because the sibling relationship itself is so underestimated, its loss is underestimated, too.

Usually, though not necessarily, an oldest or older sibling dies first. When this happens, it brings a morbid awareness of chronological order. We think about who will be next and when it will be our turn. It also alters our relationships with our surviving siblings, changing the roles we have developed with one another and leaving a gap in the family connections.

If it is a younger sibling who dies first, we feel a sense of violation of natural order. We may feel a sense of guilt because it was supposed to be we who died first. Or we may feel a sense of failure because we think we should have been able to protect our younger sibling.

If it is an only sibling who dies, we feel a sense of loneliness that we have never felt before, despite all the other people we have in our lives. Even though we certainly would rather be a survivor, we now experience the profound loneliness of that survival.

Two realizations rise to the surface as we experience the effects of a sibling's death. First, we remember that our siblings are our peers. They are not part of an older generation, as our parents were. They are part of our own generation and close to our age. Until now, we may have lulled ourselves into thinking that there was still plenty of time left for us. Now we find that time has run out for our sibling and will perhaps soon run out for us, too. Our sibling's death is a powerful and irrefutable reminder of our own vulnerability. It breaches the buffer between ourselves and our mortality. It almost carries with it a personal threat, with death feeling that much closer to us.

Second, when we lose a sibling, we lose not only that particular person but also the special role he or she played in our lives. With our parents already gone, we now lose one of the last remaining links to our past. In the case of an only sibling, it is the last and only link now gone. Who else is there who can remember us as the children we once were? Who else can recall our parents with the same kind of intimate and genuine love/hate feelings that we do? Who else can recall the experiences in our early lives that taught us special lessons, that brought us special tears and joys?

Our siblings are the only ones left who can validate our memories and confirm our pasts. Memories are what keep alive the things and people that would otherwise be lost, but it is lonely and difficult to remember them by yourself. Even when our siblings' memories do not agree with ours, or even if they are not necessarily accurate, we know that they came out of the same shared history and home. It is only with our siblings that we can remember shared experiences and with whom we share the experience of remembering.

The roots of our sibling relationships, both the positive and negative moments, go far back, into the beginnings of our lives. By now we have fought our battles, won or lost our struggles, and finally learned who we are and who we are not. We started our lives' journeys from the same place but continued down our own paths in different ways. We realize we are not necessarily like each other just because we are siblings. We also realize our siblings are special people who have irrevocably (even if unknowingly) shaped who we are, just as we have done for them. No matter if we are close or distant, if we are younger or older, if we are alike, unalike, or even liked by each other, when we lose a sibling, our own lives become diminished. We know there is no one else now, no matter how close or how caring others may be, who can bring back that part of our past and that part of ourselves that we have lost with their death.

• • •

We started out wondering what siblings really are, and we ended up finding that our relationships with them are some of the most special and lasting relationships of our lives. In our early years, we help each other begin our lives by shaping who we are and who we will become. And in our later years, we help each other close out our lives by coming to terms with each other and with our mortality.

When a sibling dies, our best consolation can be knowing (in a seemingly contradictory but comforting way) that we found each other before we lost each other. We will be able to hold dear what we have gained, and we will be able to remember our siblings not with regret but with love.

BUILDING BRIDGES
WITH YOUR SIBLINGS

1. Keep in touch, regularly or periodically, through phone calls, e-mails, postcards, or whatever you find easiest. This will subtly remind them that you care about them and that you're there for them.

2. Acknowledge and share life events, especially milestones. Don't wait for your siblings to mention your events first or worry when they don't. What you do may remind or inspire them to reciprocate.

3. Remember their children's or grandchildren's special events or achievements.(Grandchildren, especially, can be an easy and nonthreatening source of connection.)

4. Sometimes make contact for no specific reason at all, just to let them know you are thinking of them or want to share an experience or memory with them.

5. Contact them immediately if they are ill or alone or experiencing some sorrow in their lives. When you do, don't tell them about your problems or even your remedies. They don't need your advice or judgment, just your concern.

6. Be *with* them and *for* them in times of loss or serious need. Don't stand on ceremony and wait to be asked; just go there and be there. Even if there is nothing you can do, let them know you would if you could.

7. It may not be possible to forget old quarrels or differences, but don't harp on them either. Some issues may have to be relegated to the category of unfinished business.

8. If it's comfortable for you and for them, take the time to express some loving words, to offer some gestures of affection, or to give some special smiles, touches, or affirmations.

index

Aging parents, 39–43

"Best friendship," 10
Bible, 12
birth order, 20–22
building bridges,
    120–127, 133–134

Caregiving, 39–41
characteristics of sibling
    relationships,
    ambivalent, 14–15
    complicated, 13–14
    lasting, 16
    powerful, 15–16
Cinderella, 12

Death
    of parents, 41–43,
      48–49
    of siblings, *x–xi*,
      119–120, 127–130,
      131
de-identification, 28

Estrangement, 36

Firstborns, 20–21, 128
Freud, 12–13

Gender, 19, 22–24
genetic glue, 15
growing apart, 31–43,
    53–54

Health, changes in,
    x, 51–52

In-laws, 9–10, 34
interview process and
    questions, 55–56

"Kin keepers"
    parents as, 36–43
    siblings as, 49

Life review, 52–54
lifestyles, different,
    34–35

Middle children,
    21
mortality, 41–43.
    See also death
moving, 32–33
myths and messages,
    10–13

Older children.
    See firstborns

Parents
aging of, 39–43
comfort with children
by birth order, 22
death and loss of,
41–43, 48–49
decision to have
children, 17–18
expectations about
children, 18–20,
23–24, 26
gender and tempera-
ment preferences
in children, 19
influence of their history
on children, 18–20
as "kin keepers," 36–43
reactions to children,
25–26
peer relationship,
27, 128–129
personality, 20–21, 24–25

Reconnecting, 120–127,
133–134
retirement, 50–51
roles, 25–26, 37

Sex. See gender
sibling rivalry, 12–13
siblings
as adults growing apart,
31–43, 53–54
aging, 47–54

characteristics of
relationships, 13–16
in childhood, 17–29, 53
death or illness of,
119–120, 127–130, 131
defined, 9–10
finding or reconnecting
with, 119, 120–127
as first peers, 17, 27
having children of own,
34
in-law, 9–10, 34
as "kin keepers," 49
in literature, 11–12
odd or even number of,
22
same-sex or different-sex,
23, 24
shaping forces on, 20–26
stories of, 63–118
special occasions, 35, 37,
124
stories of siblings
all brothers, 59–61, 83–99
all sisters, 58–59, 63–81
mixed sisters and
brothers, 61–62,
101–118
summarized, 55–62

Temperament, 24–26
TIAs, 107

Younger siblings, 21, 128

LIFE: PART TWO® books —

As Parents Age:
A Psychological and Practical Guide
Joseph A. Ilardo, PhD, LCSW

Sensible, compassionate advice for adult children on how to talk with aging parents about the future. Self-Help Book of the Year *(ForeWord Magazine)*.

How to Enjoy Your Retirement:
Activities from A to Z (2nd edition)
Tricia Wagner and Barbara Day

More than 1000 inspiring and fun ideas for a delightful retirement. Loaded with toll-free numbers and Website addresses to help you dip into ideas quickly and inexpensively.

How to Feel GOOD As You Age:
A Voice of Experience
John Barnett

A guide to making choices that will add quality to your own present and future. The author fills this book with sensitive advice on the legal, physical, and spiritual aspects of life from midyears on.

Learning from Hannah:
Secrets for a Life Worth Living
William H. Thomas, MD

A noted gerontologist's visionary tale about a place where the wisdom of the elders offers timeless moral lessons. IPPY *(Independent Publisher)* award finalist.

(continued)

Life Worth Living:
How Someone You Love Can Still Enjoy Life in
a Nursing Home—The Eden Alternative in Action
William H. Thomas, MD

Specific guidelines for the program that fights lone-
liness, helplessness, and boredom in nursing homes.
Book of the Year in Gerontological Nursing *(American
Journal of Nursing)*.

Other books of interest —

Bring Me the Ocean:
The Natural World as Healer
Rebecca A. Reynolds

Inspirational true stories that reveal how the power
of nature and personal attention can heal emotionally
and spiritually. Multi-award winning, and the only
book on the program Animals As Intermediaries.

The Glory Walk:
A Literary Memoir
Cathryn E. Smith

A daughter's poignant tribute to her father that offers
a one-of-a-kind literary experience. Using a blend
of creative styles and unusual imagery, the author
reveals her family's memories and gives voice to the
disease that steals away her father's mind and body.

For more information
visit www.VandB.com
or call 1-800-789-7916.